THE **STIR-FRY** COOKBOOK

THE **STIR-FRY** COOKBOOK

BY GINA STEER

CONTEMPORARY BOOKS

A QUINTET BOOK

Published by Contemporary Books
A division of NTC/Contemporary Publishing Group, Inc.
4255 West Touhy Avenue, Lincolnwood (Chicago), Illinois 60712-1975
U.S.A.

Printed in China by Leefung-Asco Printers Trading Limited

International Standard Book Number: 0-8092-9304-8
01 02 03 04 05 06   15 14 13 12 11 10 9 8 7 6 5 4 3 2 1

Library of Congress Cataloging-in-Publication Data

Steer, Gina
    The stir-fry cookbook/by Gina Steer.
        p. cm.
    Includes index.
    ISBN 0-8092-9304-8
    1. Stir frying. 2. Wok cookery. I. Title.

TX689.5 .S72 2001
641. 77—dc21
                    00-65952

This book was designed and produced by
Quintet Publishing Limited
6 Blundell Street
London N7 9BH

Senior Project Editor: Toria Leitch
Editor: Anna Bennett
Designer: Deep Creative
Photographer: Ian Garlick
Food Stylist: Kathryn Hawkins
Creative Director: Richard Dewing

Typeset in Great Britain by Central Southern Typesetters, Eastbourne
Manufactured in Hong Kong by Regent Publishing Services Limited

ACKNOWLEDGMENTS

I would like to thank Juliet Barker for all her hard word in helping me test these recipes and of course I cannot forget my family who as ever have eaten every one of these dishes, commenting throughout. Also the photographer, Ian Garlick, and the food stylist, Kathryn Hawkins, who have done such a great visual job.

CONTENTS

INTRODUCTION

Welcome to the world of stir-fry cooking. Once you try it you will be instantly converted. It has to be one of the fastest ways of cooking, which is good news with today's frantic lifestyle.

Stir-fry cuisine originated in Asia, but once introduced to the West, it caught on quickly as cooks realized its vast potential. This was also helped by the popularity of Chinese food in many countries. Consumers were so impressed with the vast array of delicious and colorful dishes offered by this cuisine that they wanted to be able to reproduce these dishes for themselves at home.

The shape of the wok ensures that the heat is evenly distributed over the base of the pan. Because of this concave shape, the whole wok becomes a cooking surface. The food can be moved about inside the wok, which enables it to cook rapidly, preserving all of the valuable nutrients. It is a very healthy way of cooking because usually only a minimum amount of oil is used.

A wide range of ingredients can be cooked in a wok, and it is extremely easy to adapt Western recipes to wok cooking. The current trend toward a fusion of Eastern and Western cuisines is providing a host of recipes that are new, exciting, and suitable for all tastes and cultures. I guarantee you will find this book a valuable addition to your kitchen library.

CHOOSING AND SEASONING YOUR WOK

When choosing your wok, choose one that is large enough—14 inches in diameter is a good size. Look for one with deep sides. A heavier wok, made from carbon steel, is better than one made from light stainless steel or aluminum because the lighter ones tend to scorch. It is possible to buy electric woks with their own element, but these tend not to heat up to a sufficiently high temperature.

It is also important to choose the correct wok for your cooker. If you have an electric stove, you will need to buy a wok with a flat bottom so that the heat can be conducted through its base. A round-bottomed wok can only be used on a gas stove.

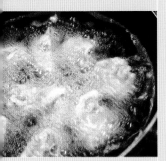

If you buy a wok with a nonstick surface you do not need to season the wok: simply wash in warm soapy water, dry thoroughly, and wipe with a little oil.

After use, cool slightly and fill with warm soapy water. Leave for a few minutes, then wipe with a sponge or cloth. Do not use a scouring powder or pad. Clean the outside of the wok regularly. Scouring pads can be used on the outside if necessary. Some nonstick woks can be put in the dishwasher but this will affect the appearance of the wok; the surface will become dull and discolored.

It is now possible to buy nonstick woks with a thermospot heat indicator. This has a red indicator in the center of the base of the wok that changes color when heating, indicating that the wok is at the correct temperature for the oil to be added and for cooking to commence.

If you buy a traditional wok you will need to season it before use. First, rinse well and scrub with a cream cleanser and water to remove the machine oil, then place on the stove over low heat. Pour in 3 tablespoons of oil. Rub this oil all over the inside of the wok with paper towels and heat on the burner for 10 to 15 minutes until really hot. Wipe with paper towels: you will find the paper will be black. Repeat this heating and wiping until the paper is clean. The wok is now ready for use. It will become darker and even more seasoned with use.

Once seasoned the wok should not be washed with detergent because this will destroy the nonstick surface. After cooking, rinse the wok under hot running water, scrub with a brush, then return to the heat to dry off. Once dry, smear with a little oil before storing.

OTHER EQUIPMENT

You will also need a few other pieces of equipment to ensure that your wok cooking is a success.

- **Wok Stand** This is a metal ring or frame that is used to keep the wok steady on the burner. It is especially useful if you want to use your wok for steaming, deep-frying, or braising.
- **Wok Lid** A domelike cover used for steaming. It may come with the wok or can be purchased separately. You can use foil instead, but make sure it fits snugly.
- **Spatula** The best type to use is a long-handled spatula rather like a small shovel, for scooping and stirring the food in the wok.
- **Rack** If you use the wok as a steamer, a wooden or metal rack is required to stand above the water level and support the plate of food to be steamed.
- **Bamboo brush** A bundle of stiff, split bamboo used for cleaning the wok without scrubbing off the seasoned surface. A soft washing-up brush would also do the job.
- **Cleavers** Food is often finely shredded in Asian cuisine. A cleaver performs this job brilliantly and can also chop up bones, herbs, vegetables, and a host of other ingredients. There are three different types: a lightweight one with a narrow blade for delicate foods; a medium weight for general cutting, chopping, and crushing; and a heavy-duty cleaver for chopping bones. Choose a good-quality cleaver and keep it well sharpened.
- **Steamers** Bamboo steamers come in a variety of sizes. To use, fill with the food to be steamed, then place on a rack in the wok, with water underneath. Clean damp cheesecloth or waxed paper can be placed over the slats on the base where the food to be cooked is placed. This prevents the food from falling through. A tight-fitting lid is placed on top. If necessary, several steamers can be placed on top of each other.

TECHNIQUES

With wok cooking it is important that a few cutting and cooking techniques are followed to ensure a good result every time.

• **Meat** should always be sliced across the grain in order to break up the fibers and make it more tender after cooking.

• **Vegetables** are better if sliced diagonally. This exposes more of the surface of the vegetable, which cooks it more quickly. To do this, angle the knife or cleaver at a slant and cut.

• **Scoring** Some foods, such as whole fish or pieces of poultry, are often scored. This means piercing the surface of the food to help the heat to penetrate more quickly and give a more attractive finish at the end of the cooking time. With a cleaver or sharp knife, make cuts at an angle across the food, taking care not to cut right through.

• **Blanching** This is covering foods with boiling water or moderately hot oil and leaving for a few minutes before draining. This softens the food so it takes less time at the final cooking. Meat is often blanched to remove any scum, thus giving a more attractive appearance and a better taste. Vegetables such as carrots or broccoli are blanched in boiling water then plunged into cold water—this reduces the final cooking time and preserves their bright color.

• **Stir-frying** Before you start to cook, it is important to have all your ingredients already prepared. Heat the wok before adding the oil (this is very important as it ensures that the food does not stick to the wok and ensures an even distribution of heat). Add the oil and heat it until it is almost smoking, unless you intend to flavor the oil. If flavoring the oil, heat the wok then add the oil and heat (but not to smoking) then add the flavoring ingredients such as chile, shallots, ginger, and lemon grass. Toss them in the oil. Then, depending on the recipe, either remove the flavoring ingredients or add the next ingredients.

• **Movement** Keep the food moving in the wok so that it cooks evenly.

• **Thickening** When thickening a dish with cornstarch at the end of cooking, take the wok off the heat and stir in the blended cornstarch, then return to the heat and cook, stirring, until thickened.

• **Draining** Any food to be deep-fried should be drained thoroughly on paper towels before cooking. If the food has been marinated, remove it with a slotted draining spoon from the marinade and allow any excess marinade to drip back into the bowl. Drain the food again after cooking on paper towels.

• **Steaming** If you are using a bamboo steamer, pour about 2 inches of water into the wok and bring to the simmering point. Place the food in the steamer, and set the steamer in the wok where it can sit safely wedged or perched on the sloping sides. Cover the steamer with its lid and steam. Add more water as necessary.

INGREDIENTS

- **Oil** The best types of oil for stir-frying are peanut or vegetable oil because they can be heated to a high temperature without burning. Do not use olive oil. Normally sesame oil is added at the end of the cooking time to add flavor and a burst of heat.
- **Flavorings** A wide variety of ingredients are used to flavor the food—garlic, ginger, galangal, (similar to ginger but with a milder citrus-pine flavor), chiles, lemon grass (which has a distinct citrus flavor), kaffir lime leaves (also with a citrus-pine flavor), fresh chopped cilantro, basil, and sesame seeds. There are also several sauces:
- **Hot chile sauce** A bright red sauce, made from chiles, sugar, salt, and vinegar. It is sometimes used in cooking, more often as a dipping sauce. There is also a sweet chile sauce which contains more sugar and is used mainly as a dipping sauce.
- **Hoisin sauce** A thick dark brown, sweet and spicy sauce made from soybeans, vinegar, sugar, and spices.
- **Oyster sauce** A thick, brown sauce made from oysters that have been cooked in soy sauce. Used as a condiment as well as in cooking.
- **Chile bean sauce** Made from soybeans and chiles. Very hot and spicy.
- **Yellow bean sauce** A thick, spicy, aromatic sauce made from yellow beans, flour, and salt, fermented together. There is also black bean sauce, made from black beans. Both are used to flavor dishes and are added during cooking.
- **Soy sauce** Both light and dark versions are used extensively in Asian cuisine as a flavoring and condiment. They are made from soy beans that have been fermented.
- **Fish sauce (*nam pla*)** Made from fermented fish, this is used in Thai foods as a seasoning. As the name implies, it has a strong fish taste.
- **Plum sauce** Made from Chinese plums which have been simmered with fresh ginger and chile, giving a sweet chile-flavored sauce with overtones of sweetness from the plums. It can be used as a dipping sauce or added to stir-fries to give a fruit and spice flavor.
- **Rice vinegar** is popular in Asian cuisine and made from rice. It can vary

from spicy and tart to sweet and pungent. There are white rice vinegars, black rice vinegars, and red rice vinegars. They can be substituted with cider or white wine vinegar.

• **Rice wine**, also known as sake is made from fermented rice. A commonly used ingredient for dressings, sauces, and marinades, it can be substituted with dry sherry.

• **Rice** and **noodles** provide the main bulk in an Asian meal. Choose from long-grain, basmati, Thai fragrant (jasmine) rice, which becomes soft and sticky on cooking, or glutinous rice, which is also known as sweet, sticky, or waxy rice (types available include Japanese, Chinese, and Thai). Normally Thai rice is served with Thai-style dishes, long-grain rice with Chinese and Indonesian dishes, and basmati is served with Indian foods.

• **Noodles** are very versatile and vary considerably. Dried noodles are usually soaked in water for up to 20 minutes, depending on the variety. Once softened the cooking time is brief. The noodles will double in bulk after soaking.

• **Mung bean noodles** are also known as bean thread or cellophane noodles; after soaking they acquire a jellylike texture.

• **Stir-fry** or **rice stick noodles** or **rice vermicelli** are thin, brittle, and semitranslucent. They can either be soaked or, if to be served crisp, fried without soaking.

• **Soba noodles** are made from buckwheat flour and are boiled before use in noodle dishes or salads.

• **Udon noodles** are thick Japanese wheat noodles normally eaten with a soy-based broth.

• **Egg noodles**, which are wheat-based, come either as slender or medium noodles and are the most widely available ones in the Western world. They can be bought both fresh and dried, and can be boiled in water as for pasta, then tossed into the stir-fry. They are either served plain or tossed with soy sauce and flavorings.

SAUCES AND PASTES

Dipping sauces and pastes are very important in Asian cuisine and can be bought or simply made at home. Try the following sauces for yourself which are some of my favorites and then when you get more adventurous, devise a few of your own.

- **Red Chile Paste** Seed 3 to 4 red bird's eye chiles and steam over a pan of simmering water for 15 minutes. Then place in a blender with 1 chopped onion, 3 crushed garlic cloves, 2 teaspoons ground coriander, 1 tablespoon grated gingerroot, the grated zest and juice of 2 limes, seasoning to taste, and 3 tablespoons oil. Blend to a thick paste, adding extra oil as required. Store in a screw-top jar in the refrigerator and use within 1 week.
- **Green Chile Paste.** Seed 3 to 4 green jalapeño chiles and place in a blender with 3 crushed garlic cloves, the chopped inside part of 3 lemon grass stalks, 6 trimmed and chopped scallions, and 2 to 3 kaffir lime leaves. Blend with 1 teaspoon honey and 2 to 3 tablespoons lime juice, then stir in 2 tablespoons chopped fresh cilantro. Store in a screw-top jar in the refrigerator for up to 1 week.

- **Ginger and Scallion Sauce** Heat the wok, add 3 tablespoons oil, and heat to almost smoking. Stir in 4 trimmed and chopped scallions, 2 teaspoons ground ginger, and 1 tablespoon light soy sauce. Once it sizzles it is ready for use.
- **Sweet-and-Sour Sauce** Blend together 3 tablespoons dark soy sauce and honey with 1 finely chopped garlic clove, 1 tablespoon rice wine, 2 teaspoons chile sauce, and a generous pinch of Chinese five-spice powder. Use as required.

When you cook an Asian meal, select just two or three dishes and serve them with some plain boiled rice or noodles. Choose dishes that harmonize in color and texture. If you like you can divide the dishes into Western-style courses, serving them as simple one-dish meals, appetizers, or hors d'oeuvres.

Before you start, read the recipe all the way through so that you are clear about the different stages. Then prepare yourself for a real taste explosion as you feast on the fabulous flavors from the East.

APPETIZERS AND
HORS D'OEUVRES

SESAME SHRIMP BALLS

THESE MAKE A DELICIOUS HORS D'OEUVRE OR APPETIZER; THEY CAN BE
PREPARED AHEAD OF TIME AND COOKED JUST BEFORE THEY ARE REQUIRED.

Makes **12 to 14**
Preparation time **15 minutes plus 1 hour**
   chilling time
Cooking time **6 to 9 minutes**

1 lb peeled shrimp, defrosted if frozen
4 scallions, trimmed and chopped
One 2-in piece gingerroot, peeled and grated
1 red jalapeño chile, seeded and chopped
2 Tbsp chopped fresh parsley
½ cup fresh white bread crumbs
Salt and freshly ground black pepper
4 Tbsp sesame seeds
Peanut oil for frying

TO GARNISH
Chopped chile and lime wedges

Dry the shrimp in paper towels, squeezing out any excess moisture, and place in a food processor with the scallions, gingerroot, chile, parsley, bread crumbs, and seasoning. Blend in short sharp bursts until the ingredients are finely chopped and blended. Chill for 30 minutes.

Place the sesame seeds in a shallow bowl. Shape the shrimp mixture into apricot-sized balls and roll them in the sesame seeds. Place on a plate, cover lightly, and chill in the refrigerator for at least 30 minutes.

Heat the wok, half-fill with the oil, and heat to 375°F. Cook the shrimp balls a few at a time for 2 to 3 minutes, or until golden and crisp. Remove from the wok with a slotted draining spoon and drain on paper towels.

Repeat until all the balls have been cooked. Serve warm, garnished with chopped chile and lime wedges.

SESAME SHRIMP TOASTS

THESE CAN BE PREPARED AHEAD OF TIME AND COOKED JUST BEFORE THEY ARE REQUIRED.

Serves **6 to 8**
Preparation time **5 minutes**
Cooking time **10 to 12 minutes**

12 oz peeled shrimp, defrosted if frozen
1 medium egg
4 scallions, trimmed and chopped fine

1 to 2 bird's eye red chiles, seeded
   and chopped fine
Freshly milled salt to taste
1 Tbsp light soy sauce
8 thin slices day-old bread
3 Tbsp sesame seeds
About 1¼ cups oil for deep-frying

Dry the peeled shrimp thoroughly on paper towels and place in a food processor with the egg, scallions, chiles, salt, and soy sauce. Blend in short sharp bursts to form a rough paste.

Spread the paste onto the pieces of bread to a depth of ½ inch and cut into small oblongs about 1 inch wide and 3 inches long. Sprinkle with the sesame seeds.

Heat the oil in the wok to 375°F and fry the sesame toasts, paste-side down, for 2 minutes, or until crisp and golden. Drain on paper towels and serve immediately.

STEAMED SCALLOPS WITH SPINACH AND RICE NOODLES

CHOOSE PLUMP, WHITE SCALLOPS, AVOIDING THOSE THAT LOOK TIRED AND GRAY.
IF BUYING FRESH AND NOT USING IMMEDIATELY, FREEZE ON THE DAY OF PURCHASE.

Soak the rice noodles in boiling water for about 4 minutes or until soft. Drain thoroughly and set aside.

Clean the scallops and place on a sheet of nonstick baking paper in the top of a bamboo steamer. Blend two of the crushed garlic cloves with the lime juice, zest, and soy sauce, and sprinkle over the scallops. Place the steamer over a wok or a large pan filled with boiling water and steam for 6 to 8 minutes, or until the scallops become opaque. Take care not to overcook or the scallops will be tough.

Meanwhile, heat the wok and add the peanut oil. When hot, stir-fry the remaining garlic and scallions for 2 minutes. Add the spinach and stir-fry for 2 minutes, or until wilted.

Add the noodles, fish sauce, and sesame oil. Stir-fry for 1 minute, or until heated through. Arrange on individual serving plates, top with the scallops, and sprinkle with the chopped cilantro before serving.

Serves **4**
Preparation time **10 minutes plus 4 minutes soaking time**
Cooking time **6 to 8 minutes**

6 oz stir-fry rice noodles

12 fresh scallops

4 garlic cloves, peeled and crushed

2 Tbsp lime juice

1 Tbsp grated lime zest

2 Tbsp light soy sauce

1 Tbsp peanut oil

6 scallions, trimmed and chopped

4 oz spinach, tough leaves and stalks discarded

1 Tbsp Thai fish sauce (nam pla)

1 tsp sesame oil

1 Tbsp chopped fresh cilantro

CHICKEN AND CORN SOUP

USE FRESH CORN ON THE COB IF POSSIBLE. THE KERNELS ARE FAR SWEETER AND CRISPER THAN FROZEN OR CANNED AND GIVE A WONDERFUL CRISP TEXTURE TO THE SOUP.

Rinse the corn cobs and discard the silky threads if necessary. Fill the wok with boiling water and add the corn cobs. Simmer gently for 15 minutes or until tender. Drain and cool before stripping off the kernels from the cobs. Set aside.

Cut the chicken into very fine shreds. Heat ⅔ cup of the chicken broth and gently poach the chicken shreds with the dried chiles for 2 minutes, or until opaque.

Add the remaining broth, the corn kernels, soy sauce, scallions, and sesame oil and simmer in the wok for 2 minutes.

Blend the cornstarch with 2 tablespoons water. Stir into the wok and cook, stirring, until the soup has thickened slightly, and serve.

Serves **4 to 6**
Preparation time **15 minutes**
  plus cooling time
Cooking time **20 minutes**

2 ears of corn on the cob, husks removed if fresh, or 1 cup fresh kernels, defrosted if frozen
8 oz boneless, skinless chicken breasts
4 cups chicken broth
½ to 1 tsp dried crushed chiles
2 to 3 Tbsp dark soy sauce
6 scallions, trimmed and chopped
1 tsp sesame oil
4 Tsp cornstarch

COCONUT AND GINGER SALMON LAKSA

THIS DELICIOUS SOUP IS INSPIRED BY THE PACIFIC RIM TREND, A STYLE OF COOKING THAT COMBINES THE BEST OF EASTERN AND WESTERN CUISINES TO PROVIDE NEW AND INNOVATIVE DISHES.

Place the egg noodles in a large bowl, cover with boiling water, and leave for 3 minutes. Drain the noodles and set aside.

Heat the wok and add the oil. When hot, gently stir-fry the garlic, ginger, chiles, and leeks for 2 minutes. Add the saffron strands, stir once, then add the salmon and stir-fry for 1 minute.

Pour in the coconut milk and broth. Bring to a boil and simmer gently for 2 minutes. Add the reserved noodles, the soy sauce, and cilantro. Return to a boil and simmer gently for 3 to 4 minutes. Blend the cornstarch with 1 tablespoon water, add to the pan, and cook for 1 minute until thickened. Sprinkle with the scallions and serve immediately.

Serves **4**
Preparation time **10 minutes**
Cooking time **10 minutes**

3 oz slender egg noodles
1 Tbsp vegetable or sunflower oil
3 garlic cloves, peeled
   and crushed
One 2-in piece gingerroot,
   peeled and grated
1 to 2 bird's eye chiles, seeded
   and sliced

2 small leeks, trimmed and sliced
A few saffron strands
8 oz salmon fillet, skinned
   and diced
1¼ cups coconut milk
2 cups fish broth
2 Tbsp light soy sauce
1 Tbsp chopped fresh cilantro
1 Tbsp cornstarch
3 scallions, trimmed and
   diagonally sliced

CRAB SPRING ROLLS

THE FILLING FOR THESE DELICIOUS ROLLS CAN CONSIST OF CHICKEN, PORK, SHRIMP, OR VEGETABLES. THEY ARE CERTAINLY WELL WORTH THE EFFORT IN MAKING.

Remove the membranes and seeds from the red bell pepper and shred fine. Set aside.

Heat the wok and add the sesame oil. Stir-fry the red bell pepper, Parma ham, chile, lime zest, scallions, and carrots for 1 to 2 minutes, or until just starting to soften. Remove and place in a bowl together with the crab meat, bean sprouts, soy sauce, and cayenne pepper. Mix well and place in a sieve or colander to drain.

Blend the flour with 2 to 3 tablespoons water to form a paste and set aside.

Place a spring roll wrapper on a work counter and place 2 to 3 tablespoons of the filling onto the wrapper. Brush the edges with a little of the flour paste and turn into the center. Roll up to form a cigar shape and seal the edge. Press firmly together to seal well. Repeat with the remaining wrappers and filling. (If using filo pastry, fold a sheet of pastry in half and then in half again, brushing the pastry with a little water before folding over. Proceed as for the spring roll wrappers, but remember that filo pastry dries out quickly, so keep it wrapped when not in use.)

Heat the wok, add the oil to a depth of about 4 inches, and heat to 375°F. Deep-fry about 3 to 4 spring rolls for about 3 minutes, turning them over as they fry, until golden and crisp. Drain on paper towels and repeat until they are all cooked. Serve warm, garnished with lime wedges and cilantro sprigs.

Makes **12**
Preparation time **20 minutes**
Cooking time **12 to 14 minutes**

1 small red bell pepper

1 Tbsp sesame oil

4 oz Parma ham, shredded

1 small green jalapeño chile, seeded and shredded fine

1 Tbsp grated lime zest

4 scallions, trimmed and shredded fine

4 oz carrots, peeled and grated

7 oz fresh or canned white crabmeat, drained if necessary

3 oz bean sprouts

1 Tbsp light soy sauce

Pinch of cayenne pepper or to taste

4 Tbsp all-purpose flour

1 package (12 to 16) spring roll wrappers (or 12 to 14 sheets filo pastry)

Vegetable or sunflower oil for deep-frying

TO GARNISH

Lime wedges and cilantro sprigs

HOT AND SOUR SOUP

TRY EATING THIS SOUP WHEN YOU ARE FEELING SLIGHTLY UNDER THE WEATHER OR HAVE THE BEGINNINGS OF
A COLD. THE CHILES IN THE SOUP HELP CLEAR THE SINUSES AND MAKE YOU FEEL BETTER.

Serves **6**

Preparation time **10 minutes plus 20 minutes soaking time**

Cooking time **7 minutes**

1/4 cup dried mushrooms

2 oz boneless, skinless chicken breast fillets

6 oz tofu (bean curd), drained

3 cups chicken broth, preferably homemade

1 to 2 bird's eye chiles, seeded and chopped

3 lemon grass stalks, bruised, outer leaves discarded

1 medium carrot, peeled and cut into thin strips

2 celery stalks, trimmed and cut into thin strips

2 to 3 Tbsp dark soy sauce

3 oz mange tout, halved

4 oz bean sprouts

2 Tbsp cornstarch

2 Tbsp dry sherry

2 Tbsp chopped fresh cilantro

Soak the mushrooms in 2/3 cup almost-boiling water for 20 minutes. Drain, setting aside the mushrooms and soaking liquid. Chop the rehydrated mushrooms into small pieces if necessary. Cut the chicken into thin strips and the bean curd into small dice. Set aside.

Heat the wok, then add the broth with the chiles and lemon grass, and simmer for 3 minutes. Add the mushrooms, soaking liquid, chicken strips, bean curd, carrot, celery, and soy sauce. Bring to a boil, and simmer for 2 minutes. Skim if necessary and add the mange tout and bean sprouts. Cook for another minute.

Blend the cornstarch with the sherry, stir into the wok, and cook, stirring, until slightly thickened. Stir in the cilantro, heat for 30 seconds, and serve.

MISO FISH SOUP

MISO SOUP IS A TRADITIONAL JAPANESE SOUP. MISO IS MADE FROM AGED AND FERMENTED SOYBEANS.

Serves **4**

Preparation time **10 minutes**

Cooking time **8 to 10 minutes**

5 cups fish or vegetable broth

One 1/2-in piece gingerroot, peeled and shredded

1 tsp mirin

1 large carrot, peeled and cut into ribbons

1 zucchini, trimmed and cut into ribbons

1 red serrano chile, seeded and chopped

8 oz firm white fish fillets

4 oz fresh salmon fillet

4 oz raw tiger shrimp, peeled

3 Tbsp miso paste

1 to 2 Tbsp soy sauce

TO SERVE

Grated daikon and fried seaweed

Place the broth in the wok with the ginger, mirin, carrots, zucchini, and chile, and bring to a boil. Simmer for 6 minutes.

Cut the fish into small pieces and add to the wok together with the raw shrimp and miso paste. Continue to simmer for 2 to 3 minutes or until the fish is done.

Add soy sauce to taste and serve in individual bowls, topped with the daikon and seaweed.

SOLE GOUJONS WITH GINGER

THE ROASTED SEASONING IN THIS RECIPE IS USED IN A VARIETY OF THE DISHES IN THIS BOOK. MAKE AND KEEP IN AN AIRTIGHT CONTAINER AND USE AS REQUIRED. THE SEASONING WILL WORK WELL WITH ALL MEAT AND POULTRY AS WELL AS FISH.

Heat a wok until hot but not smoking. Add the salt and peppercorns and stir-fry for 1 to 2 minutes, or until the salt and peppercorns begin to smoke slightly and give off a roasted aroma. Remove from the heat and cool; either grind immediately and store in a screw-top jar or store whole and grind as required.

Pour 2 tablespoons boiling water over the grated ginger and leave for 10 minutes to infuse. Drain and set aside the liquid.

Blend the sour cream or crème fraîche with the reserved ginger liquid, scallions, and chopped cilantro. Spoon into a small serving dish, cover, and store in the refrigerator until required.

Rinse the sole fillets and cut into ½-inch strips. Mix 1 teaspoon of the roasted salt and pepper mixture with the ginger and cornstarch and use to coat the sole fillets.

Heat the wok, add the oil to a depth of 4 inches, and heat to 375°F.

Deep-fry a few sole strips at a time for 1 to 2 minutes, or until golden and crisp. Drain on paper towels. Repeat until all the strips have been cooked.

Serve immediately with the ginger sauce, garnished with lemon zest, cherry tomatoes, and cilantro sprigs, if desired.

Serves **4**
Preparation time **15 minutes plus 10 minutes infusing time**
Cooking time **10 minutes**

FOR THE ROASTED SEASONING
2 oz sea salt
2 oz peppercorns

FOR THE SAUCE
One 2-in piece gingerroot, peeled and grated fine or minced
5 Tbsp sour cream or half-fat crème fraîche
3 scallions, trimmed and chopped fine
1 Tbsp chopped fresh cilantro

FOR THE FISH
1 lb sole fillets
1 tsp minced gingerroot or ½ tsp ground ginger
2 to 3 Tbsp cornstarch
Oil for deep frying

TO GARNISH
Lemon zest, cherry tomatoes, and cilantro sprigs (optional)

JUMBO SHRIMP
WITH GARLIC AND BRANDY

KEEP THE TAIL SHELL ON WHEN PEELING SHRIMP. IT LOOKS ATTRACTIVE AND
ALSO MAKES THE SHRIMP EASIER TO HOLD WHEN EATING.

Peel the shrimp, leaving the tails intact, removing the heads and the thin black vein that runs down the back. Rinse, pat dry, and place in a shallow dish. Sprinkle with the garlic, shallots, lime zest, and ginger, then add the soy sauce and Tabasco to taste. Turn the shrimp over gently to coat them lightly with the marinade ingredients. Cover and marinate in the refrigerator for 30 minutes.

When ready to cook, heat the wok and add the oil. When hot, add the shrimp and the marinade ingredients. Stir-fry for 3 to 4 minutes, or until the shrimp are done and have turned pink.

Add the brandy to the wok and heat for 30 seconds. Take the wok off the heat and either set alight and wait for the flames to subside before serving or serve immediately. Garnish with lime zest.

Serves **4 as an appetizer**
Preparation time **10 minutes plus
    30 minutes marinating time**
Cooking time **4 to 5 minutes**

16 raw jumbo shrimp
**6 garlic cloves, peeled and
    sliced fine**
**2 shallots, peeled and cut
    into thin wedges**
1 Tbsp grated lime zest
**One 1-in piece gingerroot,
    peeled and grated**
3 Tbsp light soy sauce
A few dashes Tabasco sauce
2 Tbsp sunflower or vegetable oil
3 to 4 Tbsp brandy

TO GARNISH
Lime zest

FISH AND SEAFOOD

MONKFISH WITH BOK CHOY

WHEN SOAKING DRIED MUSHROOMS, IT IS IMPORTANT TO LEAVE THEM IN THE WATER FOR AT LEAST 20 MINUTES. WHERE POSSIBLE, USE THE SOAKING LIQUID IN THE FINISHED DISH TO OBTAIN THE MAXIMUM AMOUNT OF FLAVOR.

Cover the dried mushrooms with almost-boiling water, let stand for 20 minutes, and drain, setting aside 2 tablespoons of the soaking liquid.

Trim and wipe the fish and place on a chopping board. Sprinkle with the Chinese five-spice powder and rub in lightly. Place on a plate, cover, and allow to marinate in the refrigerator for at least 1 hour.

Cut the fennel and carrot into thin strips. Thinly slice the onion. Cut the shiitake mushrooms in halves or quarters, depending on size. Shred the bok choy.

When ready to cook, remove the fish from the marinade and cut into bite-sized pieces.

Heat the wok. When hot, add the oil and stir-fry the fish for 2 minutes. Remove and set aside.

Add the prepared vegetables, except the bok choy, and then add the reserved rehydrated dried mushrooms. Stir-fry for 2 to 3 minutes.

Blend the cornstarch with the mushroom soaking liquid, the soy sauce, and rice wine or sherry.

Pour the blended mixture into the wok with the fish and bok choy. Stir-fry for 1 minute or until the fish is done and the bok choy has wilted. Serve immediately with freshly cooked rice and sprinkled with the sliced almonds.

Serves **4**
Preparation time **10 minutes plus 1 hour marinating time**
Cooking time **6 minutes**

¼ cup dried mushrooms
1 lb monkfish fillet
2 tsp Chinese five-spice powder
1 head fennel, trimmed
1 large carrot, peeled
1 medium red onion, peeled
1½ cups shiitake mushrooms, wiped
7 oz bok choy heads
1 Tbsp peanut oil
2 tsp cornstarch
2 Tbsp dark soy sauce
1 Tbsp rice wine or dry sherry

TO SERVE
Freshly cooked rice
1 Tbsp toasted sliced almonds

COD WITH WILTED SPINACH

IF SPINACH IS UNAVAILABLE, USE EITHER BOK CHOY OR CHINESE GREENS, THAT WILL
NEED TO BE SHREDDED BEFORE ADDING TO THE WOK AT THE END OF THE COOKING TIME.

Cut the cod into large cubes, place in a shallow dish, and scatter the chopped chile and garlic over the top. Blend the tomato paste with the vinegar, sherry, and orange juice, then pour over the fish. Cover lightly and marinate in the refrigerator for at least 30 minutes, turning the fish over occasionally during this time.

Discard any tough outer leaves and stalks from the spinach, wash thoroughly in plenty of cold water, and allow to drain well.

When ready to cook, drain the fish, setting aside the marinade. Heat a wok and add 1 tablespoon of the oil. When hot, stir-fry the fish for 2 to 3 minutes, or until done. Add the marinade and stir-fry for 30 seconds. Remove and keep warm.

Wipe the wok and add the remaining oil. Stir-fry the spinach in two batches, if necessary, for 2 to 3 minutes, or until just beginning to wilt. Add the scallions and orange zest, stir-fry for 30 seconds, and spoon onto a warmed serving platter. Arrange the cod on top and serve immediately.

Serves **4**
Preparation time **5 minutes plus
 30 minutes marinating time**
Cooking time **7 to 10 minutes**

1½ lb cod fillet
1 red jalapeño chile, seeded and
  chopped
2 garlic cloves, peeled and crushed
2 Tbsp tomato paste
1 Tbsp red wine vinegar
2 Tbsp medium-dry sherry
¼ cup orange juice
1½ lb spinach
2 Tbsp vegetable oil
6 scallions, trimmed and sliced
2 Tbsp grated orange zest

WARM SEAFOOD WITH
WILD MUSHROOMS

USE AS WIDE A SELECTION OF SEAFOOD AND MUSHROOMS AS POSSIBLE TO GIVE A GOOD
ASSORTMENT OF COLORS AND A GREAT RANGE OF TEXTURES.

Clean the seafood as necessary. For squid, pull the sac and tentacles apart; remove the backbone and entrails from the sac and discard the head. Rinse thoroughly. For the scallops, discard the black vein if necessary and cut in half if large. Cut the angler fish into small pieces. If using fresh shrimp, remove the heads and peel. Rinse lightly and dry on paper towels.

Heat the wok, add 1 tablespoon of the oil, and stir-fry the chile, garlic, and shallots for 2 minutes. Add the mushrooms and continue to stir-fry for 3 minutes. Remove from the wok and wipe clean if necessary.

Add the remaining oil to the hot wok and stir-fry the fish for 3 to 4 minutes. Add the mushrooms with the rice wine, soy sauce, and basil. Stir-fry for 1 minute or until the fish is done, then serve immediately with warm crusty bread and a tossed green and mixed bell pepper salad.

Serves **4**
Preparation time **15 minutes**
Cooking time **9 to 10 minutes**

1 lb fresh mixed seafood, such as squid,
   scallops, angler fish, and large shrimp
2 Tbsp peanut oil
1 red jalapeño chile, seeded and chopped
2 to 3 garlic cloves, peeled and sliced fine
4 shallots, peeled and cut into wedges
3 cups mixed wild mushrooms, such as
   chanterelles, girolles, and morels,
   wiped and sliced in half if large
2 Tbsp rice wine
2 Tbsp light soy sauce
2 Tbsp chopped fresh basil

TO SERVE
**Warm crusty bread, tossed green and
   mixed pepper salad**

SQUID WITH ASSORTED BELL PEPPERS

SQUID NEEDS ONLY A MINIMAL AMOUNT OF COOKING, ESPECIALLY IF IT IS SMALL.
IT IS BETTER TO SLIGHTLY UNDERCOOK; IF OVERCOOKED IT BECOMES CHEWY AND TOUGH.

Serves **3 to 4**
Preparation time **5 minutes**
Cooking time **5 minutes**

1 lb squid, cleaned and cut into rings
1 red bell pepper, seeded
1 yellow bell pepper, seeded
1 orange bell pepper, seeded
2 medium zucchini, trimmed
1 Tbsp sunflower or peanut oil
2 Tbsp oyster sauce
1 Tbsp hot chile sauce
6 Tbsp fish or vegetable broth
1 tsp cornstarch

TO SERVE
Thai fragrant rice

Rinse the squid thoroughly and place in a bowl. Cover with boiling water, leave for 1 minute, then drain and set aside.

Slice the peppers thinly into rings. Cut each ring in half, forming half-moon shapes. Cut the zucchini into thin strips.

Heat the wok until hot and add the oil. Stir-fry the bell peppers and zucchini for 2 minutes. Blend together the oyster and chile sauce, broth, and cornstarch, then pour into the wok and bring to a boil. Cook for 1 minute and add the squid. Stir for 1 minute, or until the squid is hot, and serve immediately with freshly cooked Thai fragrant rice.

SQUID AND ANGLER FISH STIR-FRY

IF YOU ARE LUCKY ENOUGH TO BUY YOUR SQUID STILL WITH THEIR LITTLE TENTACLES ON, USE THEM AS A GARNISH.

Serves **4**
Preparation time **10 minutes plus 30 minutes marinating time**
Cooking time **6 to 8 minutes**

8 oz prepared squid
1 lb angler fish
2 green serrano chiles, seeded and chopped
2 garlic cloves, peeled and crushed
2 Tbsp grated lime zest
4 Tbsp lime juice
1 Tbsp peanut oil
8 scallions, trimmed and diagonally sliced
6 oz sugar snap peas or mange tout
4 oz bean sprouts
1 Tbsp Thai fish sauce (nam pla)
2 Tbsp soy sauce
1 Tbsp chopped fresh cilantro
1 Tbsp roasted peanuts, optional

TO SERVE
Freshly cooked rice

Rinse the squid and cut into rings if necessary. Remove the central bone and any skin from the angler fish, and cut into small dice. Place in a shallow dish. Blend together the chiles, garlic, 1 tablespoon of the lime zest, and the lime juice. Pour over the squid and fish and allow to marinate for at least 30 minutes.

Heat the wok, add the oil, and stir-fry the squid and angler fish for 3 minutes. Add the scallions, sugar snap peas or mange tout, and continue to stir-fry for 1 minute.

Add the bean sprouts to the wok with the Thai fish and soy sauce. Stir-fry for 2 to 4 minutes or until the fish is tender, and sprinkle with the cilantro, remaining lime zest, and peanuts. Serve with freshly cooked rice.

SHRIMP WRAPS

I LOVE FAJITAS AND ENJOY USING DIFFERENT INGREDIENTS TO
CREATE A VARIETY OF FLAVORS WITHIN THE TORTILLA PANCAKES.
THESE ARE AS DELICIOUS AS THEIR MEXICAN COUSINS.

Serves **4 (makes 8 tortillas)**
Preparation time **15 minutes plus 30
  minutes marinating time**
Cooking time **5 minutes**

FOR THE SALSA

4 ripe tomatoes, seeded and chopped
2 scallions, trimmed and chopped fine
**1 jalapeño chile, seeded and
  chopped fine**
2 Tbsp lime juice
1 tsp honey, warmed
2 Tbsp chopped fresh cilantro

FOR THE WRAPS

**6 scallions, trimmed and shredded into
  matchsticks**
**One 3-in piece cucumber, peeled if
  preferred and cut into thin strips**
⅔ cup sour cream
1 Tbsp sunflower oil
12 oz raw jumbo shrimp, peeled
**4 shallots, peeled and sliced into
  thin wedges**
1 jalapeño chile, seeded and sliced thin
1 red bell pepper, seeded and sliced thin
**1 green bell pepper, seeded and
  sliced thin**
1 to 2 Tbsp dark soy sauce, or to taste
Hot chile sauce to taste
8 large wheat tortilla pancakes, warmed

Combine all the ingredients for the salsa and spoon into a small bowl. Cover and
let stand for 30 minutes to allow the flavors to develop.

Place the shredded scallions, cucumber, and sour cream in serving bowls;
cover until required.

Heat the wok and add the oil. When hot, add the jumbo shrimp, shallots,
and chile and stir-fry for 2 minutes. Add the sliced bell peppers and continue to
stir-fry for 2 to 3 minutes, or until the shrimp have turned pink. Add soy sauce
and hot chile sauce to taste. Place on a warmed serving dish and serve.

To eat, spread a warmed tortilla pancake with a little sour cream, top with the
shrimp and pepper mixture, some scallions and cucumber, and finally a spoonful
of salsa. Roll up to eat.

Shrimp Wraps

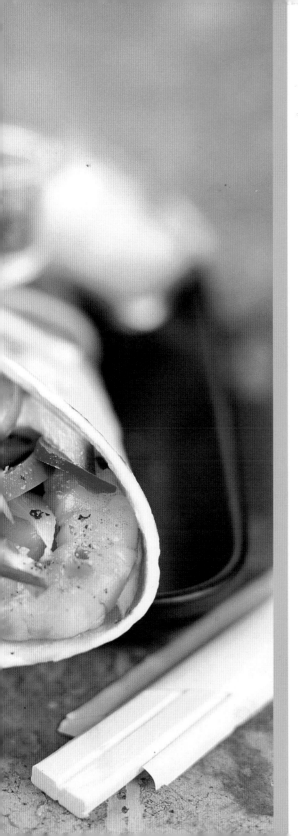

SHRIMP WITH CRISP RICE

MAKE SURE THE RICE IS THOROUGHLY DRY BEFORE FRYING.
EITHER DRY IN AN OVEN ON A BAKING SHEET OR LEAVE ON
PAPER TOWELS OVERNIGHT.

Serves **4**
Preparation time **8 minutes**
Cooking time **8 to 10 minutes**

8 oz green beans, trimmed and cut into
   small pieces
12 oz raw shrimp, peeled but
   tail shell left on
3 Tbsp cornstarch
1 large egg white
4 cups cold cooked white rice
About ½ pint oil for deep-frying

One 1-in piece gingerroot,
   peeled and shredded
1 yellow bell pepper,
   seeded and diced
One 8-oz can water chestnuts, sliced
2 Tbsp light soy sauce
2 to 4 tsp hot chile sauce, or to taste
1 tsp honey
5 Tbsp fish or vegetable broth

TO GARNISH
3 scallions, trimmed and chopped fine

Blanch the beans in boiling water for 3 minutes, drain, and set aside. Lightly rinse the shrimp and pat dry with paper towels. Blend the cornstarch with the egg white. Toss the shrimp in the egg white mixture and set aside.

Heat the oil in the wok to 375°F. Pat the rice dry with paper towels and carefully add it to the oil. (You may find it easier to do this in batches.) The rice will sizzle and puff up very quickly. Remove, drain on paper towels, and set aside.

Drain the wok, wipe clean, and reheat. Add 1 tablespoon of the drained oil and stir-fry the ginger for 30 seconds. Add the shrimp and stir-fry for 2 to 3 minutes or until they change color. Remove from the wok with a slotted spoon and set aside.

Add another tablespoon of oil and stir-fry the yellow bell pepper, green beans, and water chestnuts for 2 to 3 minutes.

Return the shrimp to the wok with the soy and chile sauces, the honey, and the broth. Stir-fry for 1 to 2 minutes, or until the beans are tender. Serve with the crisp rice, sprinkled with the scallions.

SCALLOP AND ORANGE STIR-FRY

SESAME OIL IS A THICK, RICH GOLDEN-BROWN OIL WITH A DISTINCTIVE NUTTY FLAVOR.
BECAUSE IT HEATS VERY RAPIDLY AND BURNS EASILY, IT IS OFTEN ADDED AT THE END
OF COOKING TO ROUND OFF THE FLAVOR OF A DISH.

Rinse the scallops, discard the black vein if still present, and cut in half. Place in a shallow dish and pour the soy sauce, honey, and orange juice over it. Stir lightly, cover, and allow to marinate in the refrigerator for at least 30 minutes.

Cut the broccoli into small florets and place in a bowl, cover with boiling water, let stand for 5 minutes, then drain and set aside.

Cut the celery, carrot, and orange bell pepper into thin strips and set aside.

When ready to cook, drain the scallops, setting aside 2 tablespoons of the marinade. Heat the wok until hot and add the oil. When hot, stir-fry the celery and carrot strips for 2 minutes. Add the scallops and stir-fry for 1 minute before adding the drained broccoli florets and scallions. Add the marinade and continue to stir-fry for 2 minutes, or until the scallops and vegetables are just tender. Add the sesame oil and stir lightly. Serve sprinkled with the orange zest and with freshly cooked noodles on the side.

Serves **4**
Preparation time **10 minutes**
Cooking time **5 to 7 minutes**

12 large scallops
3 Tbsp light soy sauce
1 tsp honey, warmed
2 Tbsp orange juice
6 oz broccoli florets
3 celery stalks, trimmed
1 large carrot, peeled
1 orange bell pepper, seeded
1 Tbsp sunflower or vegetable oil
6 scallions, trimmed and
  sliced diagonally
1 tsp sesame oil

TO GARNISH
Grated orange zest

TO SERVE
Freshly cooked noodles

SALMON WITH SPRING VEGETABLES

WHEN CUTTING THE SALMON INTO STRIPS, TRY TO REMOVE
AS MANY SMALL BONES AS POSSIBLE.

Serves **4**
Preparation time **10 minutes plus
  30 minutes marinating time**
Cooking time **6 minutes**

1 lb salmon fillets
1 serrano chile, seeded and chopped
1 Tbsp grated lime zest
1 Tbsp grated lemon zest
2 Tbsp lemon juice
1 Tbsp lime juice

8 oz carrots, scrubbed
4 oz mange tout
6 oz baby asparagus spears
8 oz stir-fry rice noodles
2 Tbsp peanut oil
2 Tbsp light soy sauce
2 tsp sesame oil
2 Tbsp pine nuts

TO GARNISH
Lemon and lime zest

Cut the salmon fillets into cubes, place in a shallow dish, and scatter the chopped chile over. Blend the lime and lemon zest and juices together and pour over the salmon. Cover and marinate in the refrigerator for at least 30 minutes, longer if time permits.

Cut the carrots into thin matchsticks, the mange tout and the asparagus spears in half, and set aside.

Cover the noodles with boiling water and leave for 4 minutes, or until soft. Drain and keep warm.

Heat the wok until hot and add 1 tablespoon peanut oil. Drain the salmon, setting aside the marinade, and stir-fry for 1 minute. Remove from the wok and set aside.

Add the remaining peanut oil to the wok. When hot, add the prepared vegetables and stir-fry for 2 minutes. Return the salmon to the wok with the marinade. Stir-fry for another 1 to 2 minutes, or until the fish is done. Sprinkle with the soy sauce, sesame oil, and pine nuts. Stir for 30 seconds and serve immediately with the noodles, garnished with lemon and lime zest.

Salmon with Spring Vegetables

STEAMED TROUT WITH
OYSTER SAUCE

OYSTER SAUCE IS A THICK BROWN SAUCE MADE FROM
A CONCENTRATE OF OYSTERS COOKED IN SOY SAUCE
AND BRINE. IT DOES NOT TASTE FISHY AND IS USED BOTH
IN COOKING AND AS A CONDIMENT. ONCE OPENED,
KEEP IN THE REFRIGERATOR.

Serves **4**
Preparation time **10 minutes**
Cooking time **13 to 15 minutes**

1 Tbsp peanut oil
1 to 2 tsp dried crushed chiles
2 Tbsp light soy sauce
1 Tbsp rice wine or dry sherry
3 Tbsp oyster sauce
2 Tbsp orange juice
4 small trout, cleaned

2 tsp roasted seasoning,
 (see page 24)
One 3-in piece gingerroot, peeled
 and sliced thin
2 scallions, trimmed and
 shredded fine
Grated zest of 1 orange

TO SERVE
Radish rosettes and shredded
 bok choy

Heat the wok until hot and add the oil; heat until almost smoking. Stir-fry the
chiles for 30 seconds. Add the soy sauce, rice wine or sherry, oyster sauce, and
orange juice and stir well until blended. Pour into a small pan and keep warm.
Wipe the wok clean.

Clean the trout and sprinkle the cavity with the roasted seasoning. Place the thinly
sliced ginger inside the cavities and put the trout in a bamboo steaming basket.
Scatter with a few of the shredded scallions. Cover with the lid.

Fill the wok with boiling water to a depth of 4 inches. Place the basket into
the wok and steam the trout for 12 to 15 minutes, or until done.

Remove the trout from the bamboo basket and place on a warmed serving platter.
Scatter with the remaining shredded scallion, and orange zest. Gently warm the
sauce and pour over the fish. Garnish and serve.

SEAFOOD STIR-FRY WITH
HABAÑERO SALSA

THIS SALSA WILL WORK WELL WITH MANY OF THE RECIPES IN THIS BOOK. MAKE IT AHEAD OF TIME
TO ALLOW THE FLAVORS TO DEVELOP. IF DESIRED, THE PAPAYA CAN BE SUBSTITUTED WITH MANGO.

Combine all the ingredients for the salsa and place in a serving bowl. Cover, and let stand for 30 minutes to allow the flavors to develop.

Cut the broccoli into small florets and blanch in boiling water for 5 minutes. Drain and pat dry with paper towels.

Cut the salmon into small pieces, discarding as many of the pin bones as possible. Remove the thin black vein if necessary from the scallops and cut in half if large.

Heat the wok and add the oil. Stir-fry the salmon and scallops for 1 minute. Add the broccoli and continue to stir-fry for 2 minutes, then add the soy sauce and honey. Continue to stir-fry for 1 to 3 minutes, or until the fish is done. Serve immediately with freshly cooked egg noodles.

Serves **4**
Preparation time **20 minutes**
  plus 30 minutes marinating time
Cooking time **4 to 6 minutes**

FOR THE SALSA

1 ripe papaya, peeled, seeded, and diced
4 scallions, trimmed and chopped fine
1 to 2 habañero chiles, seeded and chopped fine
3 ripe tomatoes, seeded and chopped fine
1 to 2 tsp dark brown sugar, or to taste
1 Tbsp chopped fresh cilantro
2 tsp grated lime zest

FOR THE STIR-FRY

8 oz broccoli florets
8 oz salmon fillet
8 oz scallops, cleaned
1 Tbsp peanut oil
2 Tbsp light soy sauce
1 tsp honey

TO SERVE

Freshly cooked medium egg noodles

SWEET-AND-SOUR SEA BASS

IF YOU CANNOT FIND SEA BASS FILLETS, USE OTHER FILLETS SUCH AS TROUT OR MULLET.

Soak the seaweed in lukewarm water, drain, dry thoroughly, and set aside.

Rinse the fish and pat dry with paper towels. Sprinkle the fillets with the Chinese five-spice powder and leave for 30 minutes, then coat in the cornstarch.

Meanwhile make the sauce. Place all the sauce ingredients, except the cornstarch into a small saucepan. Bring to a boil, simmer for 1 minute and blend the cornstarch with 1 tablespoon water. Stir into the sauce, and continue to stir until slightly thickened. Set aside.

Heat the oil for deep-frying in the wok to 350°F. Place the seaweed in a frying basket and deep-fry for 20 to 30 seconds, or until crisp. Drain on paper towels and set aside. Reheat the oil if necessary.

Place the carrots and zucchini in a wire basket and deep-fry for about 30 seconds, or until crisp. Remove and drain on paper towels. Deep-fry the scallions for 10 to 20 seconds, drain, and set aside. Reheat the oil if necessary.

Place 2 to 3 fillets in the hot oil and deep-fry for 3 to 4 minutes, or until crisp and golden. Drain on paper towels and keep warm. Repeat until all the fillets are cooked and reheat the sauce, if necessary. Arrange the fish fillets on a bed of seaweed on the serving plates, pour over a little of the sauce, and top with the deep-fried vegetables. Garnish with the radishes and scallions.

Serves **4**
Preparation time **10 minutes plus 30 minutes marinating time**
Cooking time **6 to 8 minutes**

1 oz dried seaweed
4 to 8 sea bass fillets, depending on size
2 tsp Chinese five-spice powder
2 Tbsp cornstarch
1 carrot, peeled and shredded
1 large zucchini, peeled and shredded
6 scallions, trimmed and shredded
About 1¼ cups oil for deep-frying

FOR THE SAUCE
1 large shallot, peeled and chopped
1 garlic clove, peeled and chopped
⅔ cup fish or chicken broth
2 Tbsp dark soy sauce
1 Tbsp tomato paste
1 Tbsp rice vinegar or white wine vinegar
1 Tbsp honey
1 to 2 tsp cornstarch

TO GARNISH
Radish rosettes and shredded scallions

DEEP-FRIED SHRIMP PLATTER

SOY SAUCE IS ONE OF THE MOST ESSENTIAL INGREDIENTS OF ASIAN COOKING. IT
IS MADE FROM A MIXTURE OF SOYBEANS, FLOUR, AND WATER THAT HAS BEEN
FERMENTED AND AGED.

Blend the soy sauce with the honey and ½ tsp of chiles and set
aside. Peel the shrimp, leaving the tail shell on but removing the
heads and the thin black vein that runs down the back of the
shrimp. Place in a shallow dish.

Blend together the remaining chiles, lemon juice, and chopped
cilantro, and pour over the shrimp. Stir lightly, cover, and marinate
in the refrigerator for 30 minutes, stirring occasionally.

Cover the broccoli florets with boiling water and leave for
10 minutes. Drain and pat dry with paper towels. Set aside.
Cut the bell peppers into ½-inch strips and set aside.

When ready to cook, beat the egg, cornstarch, and 1 tablespoon
water to form a thin batter and stir in the sesame oil. Heat the oil
in the wok to 350°F. Dip the shrimp into the batter, allowing any
excess to drip back into the bowl. Deep-fry about 4 of the shrimp
for 2 minutes, or until golden. Drain on paper towels. Repeat until
all the shrimp have been cooked.

Dip a few broccoli florets and bell pepper strips into the batter.
Deep-fry in the wok for 2 to 3 minutes, or until golden. Drain on
paper towels. Repeat until all the vegetables have been cooked.

Arrange the shrimp and vegetables on a platter and garnish with
the scallion tassels and lemon wedges. Serve with rice, a green
salad, and a small bowl of soy sauce for dipping,

Serves **4**
Preparation time **10 minutes plus**
  30 minutes marinating time
Cooking time **15 minutes**

3 Tbsp light soy sauce
1 tsp honey, warmed
1 tsp dried crushed chiles
12 oz raw jumbo shrimp
3 Tbsp lemon juice
2 Tbsp chopped fresh cilantro
6 oz small broccoli florets
1 red bell pepper, seeded
1 yellow bell pepper, seeded
1 large egg
2 Tbsp cornstarch
2 tsp sesame oil
1¼ cups oil for deep-frying

TO GARNISH
Shredded scallion and lemon wedges

TO SERVE
**Freshly cooked rice, green salad, and
  soy sauce**

LOBSTER AND MANGO MEDLEY

IF FRESH COOKED LOBSTER IS UNAVAILABLE, USE RAW SHRIMP ON THEIR OWN OR A COMBINATION OF SHRIMP AND SCALLOPS.

Serves **4**
Preparation time **8 to 10** minutes
Cooking time **6 minutes**

1 Tbsp peanut oil
½ to 1 habañero chile, seeded and chopped
One ½-in piece gingerroot, peeled and grated
1 lb cooked fresh lobster meat, cubed
10 oz fresh raw large shrimp, peeled
5 scallions, trimmed and diagonally sliced
One 3-in piece cucumber, peeled if preferred and diced
1 large ripe mango, peeled, pitted, and diced
2 Tbsp light soy sauce
2 Tbsp lime juice
1 Tbsp grated lime zest
2 Tbsp chopped fresh basil

TO SERVE
Freshly cooked Thai fragrant rice and bok choy salad

Heat the wok, add the oil, and stir-fry the chile and ginger for 1 minute. Add the lobster and/or shrimp and stir-fry for 3 minutes. Add the scallions, cucumber, and mango and stir-fry for another 2 minutes.

Add the soy sauce, lime juice, and zest, stir-fry for 1 minute, or until the shrimp are done and the lobster piping hot. Sprinkle with the basil and serve with freshly cooked Thai fragrant rice and a salad of bok choy.

ANGLER FISH WITH SPINACH AND PEPPERS

YOU CAN USE ANY WHITE FISH FILLETS, SCALLOPS, OR RAW JUMBO SHRIMP FOR THIS DISH. ONE POUND SHOULD BE ENOUGH.

Serves **4**
Preparation time **10 minutes**
Cooking time **8 to 10 minutes**

1½ lb angler fish
2 Tbsp seasoned flour
2 Tbsp peanut oil
One 2-in piece gingerroot, peeled and shredded into very thin strips
1 to 2 bird's eye chiles, seeded and shredded
2 to 4 garlic cloves, peeled and shredded thin
1 red bell pepper, seeded and shredded
1 green bell pepper, seeded and shredded
8 oz fresh spinach, shredded
1 Tbsp Thai fish sauce (nam pla)
2 Tbsp oyster sauce
1 Tbsp black bean sauce
8 oz fresh spinach, shredded
1 tsp sesame oil
4 scallions, trimmed and diagonally sliced

TO SERVE
Freshly cooked white and wild rice

Cut the fish into cubes and toss them in the seasoned flour. Set aside. Heat the wok, add 1 tablespoon of the peanut oil, and stir-fry the ginger, chiles, and garlic for 1 minute.

Add the remaining oil and stir-fry the fish for 2 to 3 minutes, or until sealed. Add the red and green bell peppers and continue to stir-fry for 2 minutes.

Blend together the fish, oyster, and black bean sauces. Pour into the wok and cook for 2 minutes. Add the spinach and stir-fry for 1 minute, or until the fish is done. Add the sesame oil and stir-fry for 30 seconds. Serve immediately, sprinkled with the scallions, with freshly cooked white and wild rice.

BEEF, PORK,
AND LAMB

STEAK STRIPS WITH BEAN PESTO

BECAUSE WOK COOKING IS SO QUICK, IT IS IMPORTANT TO BUY THE BEST-QUALITY BEEF STEAK YOU CAN—ALTHOUGH MARINATING HELPS TO TENDERIZE THE MEAT, IT CANNOT TENDERIZE CHEAPER CUTS THAT NEED LONG, SLOW COOKING.

Trim the steak and discard any fat or gristle, then cut into thin strips and place in a shallow dish. Grind some black pepper over the top. Blend 1 tablespoon of the oil with the balsamic vinegar and the red wine. Pour over the steak, cover, and marinate in the refrigerator for at least 30 minutes.

Meanwhile, make the pesto. Cook the fava beans in lightly salted boiling water for 5 minutes, or until tender. Drain and let stand until cool enough to handle. Remove the beans from their skins and place in a food processor.

Add the garlic cloves, horseradish, lemon zest, and juice and blend in short sharp bursts until a rough purée is formed. With the motor running, slowly pour in the 6 tablespoons of olive oil in a thin steady stream until a sauce consistency is formed.

Scrape into a bowl, stir in the Parmesan cheese, mix lightly, and set aside.

Heat a wok, and when really hot, add the remaining tablespoon of oil. Drain the steak and stir-fry for 2 to 4 minutes, or until done to personal preference. Remove with a slotted spoon and drain briefly on paper towels.

Either toss the cooked steak strips in the fava bean pesto until lightly coated and heat through for 30 seconds, or serve the pesto as a dipping sauce with the steak. Accompany with diced roasted potatoes, onion wedges, and garlic; garnish with rosemary sprigs.

Serves **4**
Preparation time **15 minutes plus 30 minutes marinating time**
Cooking time **10 minutes**

1 lb sirloin steak
Freshly ground black pepper
2 Tbsp olive oil
1 Tbsp balsamic vinegar
4 Tbsp red wine

FOR THE BEAN PESTO
1 cup shelled fava beans
2 to 4 garlic cloves, peeled and crushed
1 tsp grated horseradish root or creamed hot horseradish sauce
1 Tbsp grated lemon zest
2 Tbsp lemon juice
6 Tbsp extra-virgin olive oil
4 to 6 Tbsp freshly grated Parmesan cheese

TO SERVE
Diced roasted potatoes, onion wedges, and garlic

TO GARNISH
Rosemary sprigs

SPICED BEEF WITH TOMATOES

RIPE FRESH TOMATOES CAN BE USED INSTEAD OF THE CANNED TOMATOES
IN THIS RECIPE THE FLAVOR IS SUPERB.

Trim the steak, cut into thin strips and place in a shallow dish. Blend the garlic, chiles, Worcestershire sauce, and tomato paste with 2 tablespoons water. Add the sugar and pour over the steak. Cover and let stand in the refrigerator for 30 minutes, stirring occasionally.

Heat the wok and add 1 tablespoon of the oil. When hot, stir-fry the onion for 2 minutes. Remove from the wok with a slotted spoon and set aside.

Add the remaining oil to the wok and stir-fry the beef for 3 minutes. Return the onions to the wok and stir in the contents of the can of tomatoes.

Cook, stirring frequently, for 2 to 4 minutes, or until the beef is tender. Serve immediately, sprinkled with the shredded basil, with a tossed green salad and warm crusty bread.

Serves **4**
Preparation time **5 minutes plus**
30 minutes marinating time
Cooking time **9 minutes**

1 lb beef fillet or sirloin
3 large garlic cloves, crushed
1 tsp dried crushed chiles
1 Tbsp Worcestershire sauce
1 Tbsp tomato paste
1 tsp sugar
2 Tbsp oil
1 onion, peeled and sliced
One 14-oz can chopped tomatoes
2 Tbsp shredded fresh basil

TO SERVE
**Tossed green salad and warm
 crusty bread**

TERIYAKI BEEF STIR-FRY

DARK SOY SAUCE HAS BEEN AGED LONGER THAN LIGHT SOY SAUCE AND IS SLIGHTLY THICKER AND STRONGER—IT IS IDEAL TO USE AS A DIPPING SAUCE.

Serves **4**
Preparation time **10 minutes**
  plus 30 minutes marinating time
Cooking time **5 minutes**

1 lb sirloin steak
4 Tbsp dark soy sauce
4 Tbsp mirin
2 Tbsp sake or sherry
4 oz sugar snap peas
1 red bell pepper, seeded

4 oz baby asparagus
1 Tbsp sunflower oil

TO GARNISH
1 bird's eye chile, sliced thin
  and seeded

TO SERVE
Freshly cooked Thai
  fragrant rice

Trim the steak, discarding any fat. Slice thin into flat slices, rather than strips, and place in a shallow dish. Blend the soy sauce, mirin, and sake and pour over the steak. Cover and marinate in the refrigerator for at least 30 minutes. Spoon the marinade over occasionally during this time.

Trim the sugar snap peas, slice the red bell pepper into thin strips, and trim the bases from the asparagus spears and cut into 2-inch lengths.

When ready to cook, drain the steak, keeping 2 tablespoons of the marinade to one side. Heat the wok and add the oil. Add the prepared vegetables and stir-fry for 1 minute. Remove from the wok and set aside.

Add the drained beef to the wok and stir-fry for 2 minutes. Return the vegetables to the wok with the reserved marinade. Stir-fry for 1 to 2 minutes, or until the beef is done to personal preference and the vegetables are hot but still crisp.

Serve the beef, sprinkled with the chile, with the Thai fragrant rice.

BEEF STRIPS WITH EGGPLANT

CUT THE EGGPLANT FOR THIS RECIPE INTO SMALL CUBES TO ENSURE THAT THEY ARE COOKED THOROUGHLY.

Serves **4**
Preparation time **10 minutes**
Cooking time **9 to 11 minutes**

1 lb beef steak, such as sirloin
  or rump
2 Tbsp peanut oil
1 eggplant, trimmed and diced
8 oz green beans, trimmed,
  halved, and blanched

1 red bell pepper, seeded and
  cut into thin strips
3 tomatoes, seeded and chopped
4 Tbsp hoisin sauce
2 Tbsp light soy sauce
1 tsp sesame oil
1 Tbsp chopped fresh
  flat-leaf parsley

Trim the beef if necessary and cut into thin strips. Heat the wok, add 1 tablespoon of the peanut oil, and stir-fry the beef strips for 2 minutes or until sealed. Remove from the wok with a slotted spoon and set aside.

Add the remaining oil and stir-fry the eggplant for 3 minutes. Add the beans and red bell pepper and stir-fry for 2 minutes.

Return the beef to the wok together with the tomatoes, hoisin, and soy sauce. Continue to stir-fry for 2 to 4 minutes, or until the beef is tender and the vegetables are done but still crisp.

Add the sesame oil, give a final stir, then sprinkle with the parsley and serve.

THAI BEEF PARCELS

CHILES ARE USED EXTENSIVELY IN ASIAN COOKERY—THE BIRD'S EYE CHILE IS EXTREMELY HOT, SO REMEMBER TO TAKE CARE WHILE HANDLING AND DO WASH YOUR HANDS THOROUGHLY AFTERWARDS BEFORE TOUCHING ANY PARTS OF THE BODY.

Trim the beef, cut into thin matchsticks, and place in a shallow dish. Scatter the chile, garlic, lemon grass, and galangal or ginger over the top. Blend the lime juice with 1 tablespoon of the oil, pour over the beef, and stir until coated. Cover and let stand in the refrigerator for at least 30 minutes.

Meanwhile, make the dipping sauce by combining all the ingredients together. Let stand for about 20 minutes to allow the flavors to develop.

Place the cilantro, cucumber, scallions, and peanuts in small serving dishes and the lettuce leaves in a basket.

When ready to serve, drain the beef and heat the wok until hot, then add the remaining oil. When hot, stir-fry the beef for 2 to 3 minutes, or until done to personal preference. Arrange on a warmed serving platter. Serve with the dipping sauce and accompaniments.

To eat, place a lettuce leaf on a plate, fill with a spoonful of beef, and add a few of the accompaniments. Sprinkle on a little dipping sauce, fold over, and eat.

Makes **8 parcels**
Preparation time **20 minutes**
   plus 30 minutes marinating time
Cooking time **3 minutes**

10 oz sirloin steak
1 to 2 bird's eye chiles, seeded
  and chopped
2 to 3 garlic cloves, peeled
  and crushed
2 lemon grass stalks, chopped,
  outer leaves discarded
One 1-inch piece galangal or
  gingerroot, peeled and grated
3 Tbsp lime juice
2 Tbsp sunflower oil

FOR THE DIPPING SAUCE
3 Tbsp light soy sauce
1/4 tsp hot pepper sauce,
  or to taste
2 tsp honey, warmed

TO SERVE
2 Tbsp chopped fresh cilantro
One 4-in piece cucumber,
  peeled if preferred and
  cut into thin matchsticks
6 to 8 scallions, trimmed
  and shredded
1/2 cup roasted peanuts, chopped
8 to 10 whole large iceberg
  lettuce leaves, lightly rinsed

ASIAN BEEF

POUND THE STEAK WITH A MEAT MALLET TO TENDERIZE IT BEFORE CUTTING INTO STRIPS.

Cut the beef steak into thin strips and set aside. Heat the wok and add 1 tablespoon of the oil. When hot, stir-fry the beef for 2 minutes, or until sealed. Remove from the wok with a slotted spoon and set aside.

Add the remaining oil to the wok and stir-fry the garlic, celery, and carrot for 2 minutes. Add the asparagus and stir-fry for 1 minute.

Return the beef to the wok with the chile paste and cook for 2 minutes, stirring throughout. Blend the coconut milk and cornstarch together, add to the wok and cook, stirring, until the sauce has thickened and the beef is tender. Sprinkle with the cilantro. Serve with the rice, garnished with chile flowers.

Serves **4**
Preparation time **10 minutes**
Cooking time **9 minutes**

1¼ lb beef steak, such as
   sirloin or fillet
2 Tbsp peanut oil
2 to 3 garlic cloves, peeled
   and chopped
4 celery sticks, trimmed and
   cut into sticks
2 carrots, peeled and cut into
   thin sticks
4 oz baby asparagus, trimmed
   and cut in half
2 Tbsp green chile paste
   (see page 12)
⅔ cup coconut milk
1 tsp cornstarch
2 Tbsp chopped fresh cilantro

TO SERVE
Freshly cooked rice

TO GARNISH
Chile flowers

FIVE-SPICE LAMB

BUY BEAN SPROUTS THE DAY YOU INTEND TO USE THEM AS THEY DO NOT KEEP VERY WELL.

Serves **4**
Preparation time **10 minutes**
Cooking time **7 to 8 minutes**

6 oz medium egg noodles

1 lb lean lamb, such as leg steaks

2 Tbsp peanut oil

4 shallots, peeled and cut into wedges

3 garlic cloves, peeled and sliced

1 bird's eye chile, seeded and chopped

1 red bell pepper, seeded and sliced into half-moons

1 large zucchini, trimmed and cut into thin strips

2 tsp Chinese five-spice powder

1 Tbsp dark soy sauce

1 Tbsp honey

3 Tbsp lamb or chicken broth

1 tsp cornstarch

4 oz bean sprouts

6 scallions, trimmed and diagonally sliced

Cook the noodles in boiling water for 4 minutes, or according to the package instructions. Drain and set aside.

Trim the lamb if necessary and cut into small strips. Heat the wok, add 1 tablespoon of the oil, and stir-fry the lamb for 3 minutes or until sealed. Remove from the wok and set aside.

Add the remaining oil to the wok and stir-fry the shallots, garlic, and chile for 1 minute. Add the red bell pepper and zucchini and continue to stir-fry for 2 minutes. Then return the lamb to the wok.

Blend the Chinese five-spice powder with the soy sauce, honey, broth, and cornstarch and stir into the wok. Cook, stirring, then stir in the reserved noodles and the bean sprouts. Cook for 1 to 2 minutes or until the lamb is tender, then serve sprinkled with the scallions.

THAI-STYLE SPICY PORK

WHEN I SERVED THIS TO MY DAUGHTER WHO HAS TRAVELED EXTENSIVELY IN ASIA, SHE THOUGHT IT TASTED AS AUTHENTIC AS ANY DISH SHE HAD EATEN ON HER TRAVELS.

Serves **4**
Preparation time **8 minutes**
Cooking time **7 to 8 minutes**

1 Tbsp peanut oil

2 shallots, peeled and chopped

2 garlic cloves, peeled and chopped

1 lemon grass stalk, chopped, outer leaves discarded

1 to 2 bird's eye chiles, seeded and chopped

2 Tbsp grated gingerroot

2 kaffir lime leaves

8 oz fresh pork fillet, cut into thin strips

6 oz baby asparagus spears, halved

1 yellow bell pepper, seeded and sliced

1 Tbsp Thai fish sauce (nam pla)

2 Tbsp plum sauce

3 Tbsp coconut milk

8 scallions, trimmed and chopped

2 Tbsp chopped fresh cilantro

TO SERVE
Freshly cooked noodles

Heat the wok, add the oil, and stir-fry the shallots, garlic, lemon grass, chiles, and gingerroot for 1 minute. Add the lime leaves and pork and continue to stir-fry for 2 to 3 minutes, or until the pork is sealed.

Add the asparagus and yellow bell pepper strips and continue to stir-fry for 2 minutes. Stir in the fish and plum sauce with the coconut milk, stir-fry for 2 minutes, then add the scallions and chopped cilantro and serve with the noodles.

LAMB WITH RED BELL PEPPERS AND CHERRY TOMATOES

LAMB FILLET IS IDEAL FOR STIR-FRYING BECAUSE THE FAT IN IT HELPS TO MAKE THE MEAT TENDER, AND ALSO GIVES IT A REALLY GOOD FLAVOR.

Serves **4**
Preparation time **10 minutes plus 30 minutes**
  marinating time
Cooking time **8 minutes**

1 lb lamb fillet
4 garlic cloves, peeled and crushed
2 Tbsp sunflower oil
4 Tbsp chopped fresh flat-leaf parsley
1 Tbsp tomato paste
3 Tbsp orange juice
2 red bell peppers, seeded and sliced thin
¾ cup cherry tomatoes, halved
¼ cup pitted black olives, halved
Salt and freshly ground black pepper

TO SERVE
Fresh arugula leaves

Trim off any excess fat from the fillet, cut into thin strips, and place in a shallow dish. Blend the garlic with 1 tablespoon oil, 2 tablespoons parsley, the tomato paste, and the orange juice, then pour over the lamb. Turn the fillet. Cover and marinate in the refrigerator for at least 30 minutes.

Heat the wok until hot, add the remaining 1 tablespoon oil, and stir-fry the bell peppers for 2 minutes. Remove from the wok.

Add the lamb and marinade to the wok and stir-fry for 3 minutes before returning the bell peppers to the wok. Stir-fry for 60 seconds and add the cherry tomatoes and olives. Stir-fry for 1 to 2 minutes or until the lamb is tender. Add seasoning to taste and serve on a bed of arugula leaves, sprinkled over with the remaining parsley.

THAI BEEF CURRY

LEMON GRASS IS A LONG SLIM BULB WITH A DISTINCTIVE LEMON-CITRUS FLAVOR. CUT OFF THE ROOT TIP AND PEEL AWAY THE TOUGH OUTER LAYERS OR LEAVES. LEMON GRASS WILL KEEP FOR SEVERAL DAYS IN A COOL PLACE AND CAN BE CHOPPED AND FROZEN.

Serves **4**
Preparation time **5 minutes**
Cooking time **9 minutes**

1 Tbsp oil
3 Tbsp red chile paste
  (see page 12)
2 lemon grass stalks, chopped, outer
  leaves discarded
1 lb beef fillet or sirloin,
  trimmed and cubed
1 green bell pepper, seeded and
  cut into strips
1 red bell pepper, seeded and
  cut into strips
⅔ cup beef broth
2 Tbsp lime juice
1 to 2 tsp Thai fish sauce (nam pla)
1 to 2 tsp dark brown sugar

TO GARNISH
2 Tbsp roasted peanuts, chopped
1 Tbsp chopped fresh cilantro

TO SERVE
Freshly cooked Thai fragrant rice

Heat the wok then add the oil and stir-fry the red chile paste and lemon grass over a low heat for 2 minutes. Increase the heat slightly then add the beef and stir-fry for 3 minutes.

Add both the bell peppers and continue to stir-fry for 2 minutes before adding the broth, lime juice, fish sauce, and sugar. Continue to stir-fry for 2 minutes or until the beef is tender.

Serve, sprinkled with the chopped peanuts and cilantro, with the freshly cooked rice.

CHILE LAMB

PEANUT OIL IS WIDELY USED IN ASIAN COOKING, BECAUSE IT HAS A MILD, PLEASANT TASTE AND CAN BE HEATED TO A HIGHER TEMPERATURE THAN OTHER OILS, WHICH MAKES IT PERFECT FOR DEEP- AND STIR-FRYING. IF YOU CANNOT FIND THIS OIL, USE EITHER CORN OR SUNFLOWER OIL.

Discard any excess fat or gristle from the lamb, cut into thin strips, and place in a shallow dish. Blend the garlic, chiles, cilantro, lime juice, tomato paste, and 1 tablespoon of the oil and pour over the lamb. Stir well, cover, and marinate in the refrigerator for 30 minutes. Stir occasionally during this time.

Place the green bell pepper in a small bowl, cover with boiling water and let stand for 5 minutes, then drain and set aside.

When ready to cook, heat the wok and add the remaining oil. Stir-fry the lamb for 3 minutes, then add the drained green bell pepper and the kidney beans and stir-fry for 2 minutes.

Meanwhile cover the noodles with boiling water, leave for 4 minutes, then drain and keep warm.

Add the cherry tomatoes to the wok and stir-fry for 2 to 3 minutes, or until the tomatoes have began to break up and the lamb is tender. Add seasoning to taste. Serve the lamb with the noodles and the sour cream, salsa, and grated cheese.

Serves **4**
Preparation time **10 minutes plus 30 minutes marinating time**
Cooking time **8 minutes**

1 lb lamb fillet
3 garlic cloves, peeled and crushed
1 to 2 red serrano chiles, seeded and chopped
1 tbsp chopped fresh cilantro
2 Tbsp lime juice
2 Tbsp tomato paste
2 Tbsp peanut oil
1 green bell pepper, seeded and chopped
One 14-oz can red kidney beans, drained and rinsed
8 oz medium egg noodles
1 cup cherry tomatoes, halved
Salt and freshly ground black pepper

TO SERVE
Sour cream, salsa, grated Cheddar or Monterey Jack cheese

LAMB LIVER WITH RED BELL PEPPER AND SHERRY

LIVER IS IDEAL COOKING IN A WOK AS IT ONLY NEEDS A MINIMUM OF COOKING, AND WITH A
WOK THERE IS LESS DANGER OF THE LIVER BEING OVERCOOKED.

Serves **4**
Preparation time **10 minutes**
Cooking time **8 minutes**

6 oz broccoli florets

1 lb lamb liver

2 Tbsp cornstarch

2 Tbsp oil

1 red onion, peeled and sliced into rings

1 red bell pepper, seeded and cut into
   half-moon slices

2 garlic cloves, peeled and sliced

3 Tbsp medium-dry sherry

2 Tbsp light soy sauce

1 tsp honey

Cover the broccoli with boiling water and leave
for 5 minutes, then drain and set aside.

Discard any tubes from the liver and cut into
strips, rinse lightly, and pat dry on paper towels.
Coat in the cornstarch and set aside.

Heat the wok and add 1 tablespoon of the oil. Then
add all the vegetables, including the garlic, and
stir-fry for 3 minutes. Remove with a slotted
draining spoon and set aside.

Add the remaining oil to the wok and stir-fry the
lamb liver for 2 minutes. Return the vegetables
to the wok and stir-fry for 2 minutes before adding
the sherry, soy sauce, and honey; stir-fry for 1
minute. Serve immediately.

LAMB STIR-FRY
WITH OYSTER SAUCE

THIS COLORFUL DISH WOULD BE PERFECT FOR AN
INFORMAL SUPPER OR LUNCH.

Serves **4**
Preparation time **10 minutes**
Cooking time **10 to 11 minutes**

1 lb lean lamb

1 Tbsp roasted seasoning
   (see page 24)

1 Tbsp peanut oil

1 red onion, peeled and cut into wedges

2 to 4 garlic cloves, peeled and
   sliced thin

1 red bell pepper, seeded and

sliced thin

1 orange bell pepper, seeded
   and sliced thin

2 Tbsp light soy sauce

4 Tbsp oyster sauce

7 oz bok choy, shredded

6 scallions, trimmed and
   diagonally sliced

TO SERVE
Freshly cooked noodles

Trim the lamb of all its fat and cut into thin strips. Place in a plastic bag
with the seasoning and toss until lightly coated.

Heat the wok and add the oil. When hot, stir-fry the lamb for 4 minutes. Add
the onion and garlic and continue to stir-fry for 1 minute.

Add the red and orange bell peppers and continue to stir-fry for 3 minutes
before adding the soy and oyster sauce. Stir-fry for 1 to 2 minutes, or until
the lamb is tender, then add the shredded bok choy and cook for 1 minute.
Sprinkle with the scallions and serve with the noodles.

HONEYED PORK

WHEN USING HONEY IN A RECIPE FOR A MARINADE, IT IS ALWAYS A GOOD IDEA TO WARM THE HONEY BRIEFLY BEFORE MEASURING IT OUT. YOU CAN EITHER DO THIS IN A MICROWAVE FOR A FEW SECONDS, OR IF THE OVEN IS ON, PLACE THE JAR ON THE OVEN SHELF. ALTERNATIVELY, PLACE THE JAR IN A BOWL AND POUR SOME BOILING WATER AROUND IT TO COME HALFWAY UP THE SIDES. LET STAND FOR ABOUT 1 MINUTE, THEN USE.

Cut the pork into thin strips and place in a shallow dish. Blend the honey, hoisin sauce, ginger, and crushed garlic with 2 tablespoons boiling water and pour over the pork. Cover and marinate for 30 minutes in the refrigerator.

Heat the wok, add the oil, and stir-fry the pork for 2 minutes, or until sealed. Add the carrot to the wok and continue to stir-fry for another 2 minutes before adding the mushrooms, soy sauce, and rice wine or dry sherry.

Stir-fry for 2 minutes, and then add the shredded bok choy, the water chestnuts, and the bamboo shoots. Cook for another 1 to 2 minutes, or until the pork is tender. Add the parsley and serve with freshly cooked noodles.

Serves **4**
Preparation time **8 to 10 minutes plus 30 minutes marinating time**
Cooking time **7 to 8 minutes**

1 lb pork fillet
2 Tbsp honey
1 Tbsp hoisin sauce
1 Tbsp grated gingerroot
1 garlic clove, peeled and crushed
1 Tbsp peanut oil
2 carrots, peeled and cut into matchsticks
1½ cups shiitake mushrooms, wiped and sliced
2 Tbsp light soy sauce
1 Tbsp rice wine or dry sherry
7 oz bok choy, shredded
One 8-oz can water chestnuts, drained
One 8-oz can bamboo shoots, drained
1 Tbsp chopped fresh flat-leaf parsley

TO SERVE
Freshly cooked noodles

STIR-FRIED PORK WITH MANGO

FRESH GINGERROOT IS A STAPLE INGREDIENT IN ASIAN CUISINE. IT IS ESPECIALLY USEFUL WHEN COOKING SEAFOOD AS IT HELPS TO NEUTRALIZE FISH ODOR. KEEP IN THE REFRIGERATOR FOR UP TO 2 WEEKS, WRAPPED IN PLASTIC WRAP.

Serves **4**
Preparation time **10 minutes**
  plus 30 minutes marinating time
Cooking time **8 minutes**

1 lb pork fillet
One 2-in piece gingerroot,
  peeled and grated
1 green jalapeño chile, seeded
  and chopped
2 large garlic cloves, peeled
  and crushed
5 Tbsp mango or orange juice
2 Tbsp dark soy sauce
2 Tbsp oil

6 shallots, peeled and cut
  into fine shreds
2 zucchini, trimmed and
  cut into strips
1 red bell pepper, seeded and
  cut into thin strips
1 ripe but firm mango, peeled,
  pitted, and cut into strips

TO GARNISH
Grated orange zest

TO SERVE
Freshly cooked white rice

Trim the pork, cut into strips, and place in a shallow dish. Scatter the ginger, chile, and garlic over the pork, then pour over the fruit juice, soy sauce, and 1 tablespoon of the oil. Cover and leave in the refrigerator for 30 minutes, stirring occasionally. Drain the pork and set aside the marinade.

When ready to serve, heat the wok and add the remaining oil. When heated, stir-fry the pork for 4 minutes. Add the shallots, zucchini, and red bell pepper and stir-fry for 2 minutes. Add the mango and stir-fry for 1 minute, or until the pork is tender.

Add the remaining marinade, stir-fry for 1 minute, then sprinkle with the orange zest and serve with the rice.

SWEET-AND-SOUR PORK BITES

USE PORK FILLET FOR THIS DISH AND CUT INTO BITE-SIZE PIECES, TRIMMING OFF ANY EXCESS FAT OR SINEW.

Trim the pork, cut into small cubes, and place in a shallow dish. Blend the soy sauce with the roasted seasoning and the vinegar. Pour over the pork, stir, cover, and marinate in the refrigerator for at least 30 minutes. Stir the pork a few times while marinating. Heat the oil in the wok to 375°F.

Meanwhile, beat the egg, then beat in the cornstarch until a thin batter is formed. Remove the pork from the marinade and coat, a few pieces at a time, in the batter. Fry in the hot oil for 3 minutes, or until golden and cooked. Drain on paper towels. Repeat until all the pork has been cooked. Place in a serving dish and keep warm.

Place all the sauce ingredients in a medium-sized pan, stirring well to blend in the cornstarch. Place over a moderate heat and cook, stirring, until slightly thickened. Serve with the pork, garnishing with the chives.

Serves **4**
Preparation time **10 minutes**
  plus 30 minutes marinating time
Cooking time **12 minutes**

12 oz lean pork
1 Tbsp light soy sauce
½ to 1 tsp roasted seasoning,
  or to taste (see page 24)
1 Tbsp rice wine or sherry
1 medium egg
2 Tbsp cornstarch
Peanut or sunflower oil for
  deep-frying

FOR THE SAUCE
½ small red bell pepper, seeded
  and cut into thin strips

1 small carrot, peeled, cut into
  thin ribbons
1 Tbsp sherry vinegar
1 Tbsp tomato paste
1 Tbsp soy sauce
1 tsp light brown sugar
½ cup chicken broth
1 tsp honey
1 to 2 tsp cornstarch

TO SERVE
Freshly cooked rice

TO GARNISH
Chives

PORK WITH GREEN VEGETABLES
AND CRISP NOODLES

IT IS AMAZING TO WATCH THESE NOODLES PUFF UP IN THE HOT OIL. DO TAKE CARE THOUGH: IF YOU LEAVE THEM IN FOR TOO LONG, THEY QUICKLY GET BURNT.

Blanch the broccoli in boiling water for 5 minutes, then drain and set aside.

Heat the oil for deep-frying in the wok to 375°F. Carefully place a few noodles in the oil for 10 to 20 seconds or until puffed up and golden, then remove and drain. Repeat until all the noodles are cooked.

Trim the pork, cut into thin strips, and set aside. Heat the wok, then add 1 tablespoon of the peanut oil and stir-fry the garlic, ginger, and lemon grass for 1 minute. Add the remaining peanut oil and stir-fry the pork until sealed. Add the broccoli and continue to stir-fry for 2 minutes.

Add the remaining vegetables and stir-fry for 2 to 3 minutes, then add the soy sauce, fish sauce, and honey. Stir-fry for 2 minutes, or until the pork is tender and the vegetables are done but still crisp. Serve with the crisp noodles.

Serves **4**
Preparation time **15 minutes**
Cooking time **8 to 9 minutes**

6 oz broccoli florets

2 cups oil for deep-frying

2 to 3 oz cellophane (transparent stir-fry) noodles

1 lb pork fillet

2 Tbsp peanut oil

2 garlic cloves, peeled and chopped

One 2-in piece gingerroot, peeled and shredded

1 lemon grass stalk, chopped, outer leaves discarded

1 small zucchini, trimmed and cut into strips

4 oz sugar snap peas or mange tout

8 scallions, trimmed and diagonally sliced

2 Tbsp light soy sauce

1 Tbsp Thai fish sauce (nam pla)

1 tsp honey

PORK WITH BLACK BEAN SAUCE

ASIAN COOKERY INVOLVES A NUMBER OF THICK, FLAVORFUL SAUCES SUCH AS BLACK BEAN SAUCE. IT IS MADE FROM SALTED BLACK BEANS OR BLACK SOYBEANS WHICH HAVE BEEN FERMENTED WITH SALT AND SPICES. THE SAUCE HAS A DISTINCTIVE, SLIGHTLY SALTY TASTE WITH A HINT OF GARLIC AND FRESH GINGER.

Trim the pork and cut into very thin strips. Blend the soy sauce with the orange juice and cornstarch in a large bowl. Add the pork and toss until coated. Cover lightly and let stand in the refrigerator for at least 30 minutes to marinate.

Heat the wok until hot and add 1 tablespoon of the oil. When hot, stir-fry the garlic for 30 seconds. Add the pork and stir-fry for 2 minutes. Remove from the wok and set aside.

Wipe the wok clean if necessary and heat the remaining oil, then add the carrot, 2 scallions, green beans, and cucumber and stir-fry for 2 minutes. Return the pork to the wok, add the black bean sauce, and stir-fry for 1 to 2 minutes, or until the pork is tender.

Serve with the freshly cooked noodles, sprinkled with the remaining scallions.

Serves **4**
Preparation time **10 minutes plus 30 minutes marinating time**
Cooking time **5 to 6 minutes**

1 lb pork fillet
1 Tbsp light soy sauce
1 Tbsp orange juice
1 tsp cornstarch
2 Tbsp peanut or sunflower oil
3 garlic cloves, peeled and sliced thin
1 large carrot, peeled and cut into very thin strips
3 scallions, trimmed and sliced
4 oz green beans, trimmed and halved
One 3-in piece cucumber, peeled if preferred and cut into strips
3 to 4 Tbsp black bean sauce

TO SERVE
Freshly cooked medium egg noodles

PORK SPRING ROLLS

IF PREFERRED YOU CAN REPLACE THE BEAN SPROUTS WITH THE SAME AMOUNT OF FINELY
SHREDDED BOK CHOY.

Cut the pork into very fine strips and place in a shallow dish.
Blend together the soy sauce, rice wine or sherry, and cornstarch.
Pour over the pork and let stand for 30 minutes.

Heat the wok, add the peanut oil, and stir-fry the pork for
1 minute. Add the sesame oil, chile, and vegetables and stir-fry for
another 2 to 3 minutes. Remove and cool.

Blend the flour with 2 to 3 tablespoons water to form a paste,
then place a spring roll wrapper on the work counter and place
2 to 3 tablespoons of the filling on the wrapper. Brush the edges
with a little of the flour paste and turn the edges into the center.
Roll up to encase the filling and seal the edge with the flour paste.
Press the edges firmly. Repeat until all the wrappers and filling
have been used. (If using filo pastry, fold a sheet of pastry in half
and then in half again, brushing the pastry with a little water before
folding. Proceed as for spring roll wrappers.)

Heat the wok, add the oil for deep-frying, and heat to 375°F. Deep-
fry 3 to 4 rolls at a time for 3 minutes or until crisp. Turn the rolls
over during cooking. Drain well on paper towels. Repeat until all the
rolls are cooked, and serve warm.

Serves **4 to 6**
Preparation time **20 minutes plus**
   30 minutes marinating time
Cooking time **12 to 16 minutes**

8 oz lean pork fillet
2 Tbsp soy sauce
1 Tbsp rice wine or dry sherry
1 tsp cornstarch
1 Tbsp peanut oil
1 Tbsp sesame oil
1 bird's eye chile, seeded and
   chopped fine
1 orange bell pepper, seeded
   and cut into thin shreds
4 oz carrot, peeled and grated
3 oz bean sprouts
4 oz water chestnuts, shredded
4 Tbsp all-purpose flour
1 package spring roll wrappers
   or about 12 sheets filo pastry
Peanut oil for deep-frying

POULTRY
AND GAME

FRAGRANT CHICKEN

KAFFIR LIME LEAVES ARE SMOOTH, DARK GREEN LEAVES WITH AN INTENSELY AROMATIC CITRUS-PINE FLAVOR. THEY CAN BE FROZEN AND CAN BE BOUGHT DRIED AS WELL. IF UNAVAILABLE, USE GRATED LIME ZEST.

Make 3 diagonal slashes across each chicken breast and place in a shallow dish.

Place the lemon grass, cardamom pods, dried crushed chiles, lime leaves, scallions, star anise, and cilantro in a food processor and blend to a chunky purée or pound to a purée in a mortar and pestle. Stir in the lime zest and juice and spread over the chicken breast. Cover and let stand in the refrigerator for 30 minutes.

Heat the wok and add the oil. When hot, cook the chicken for 5 minutes, turning frequently, until browned. Add the broth, reduce the heat, and cover with either a lid or large piece of foil.

Cook for 15 minutes, or until the chicken is thoroughly cooked. Serve with the cooking juices spooned over and garnished with the chile and scallions.

Serves **4**
Preparation time **5 minutes plus 30 minutes marinating time**
Cooking time **20 minutes**

4 boneless, skinless chicken breast fillets
3 lemon grass stalks, chopped, outer leaves discarded
6 cardamom pods, lightly crushed
½ to 1 tsp dried crushed chiles
3 kaffir lime leaves, crushed if using dried leaves
6 scallions, trimmed and chopped
3 star anise
1 Tbsp chopped fresh cilantro
1 Tbsp grated lime zest
2 Tbsp lime juice
1 Tbsp oil
1 cup chicken broth

TO GARNISH
Shredded chile and chopped scallions

CHICKEN WITH PEANUT SAUCE

PALM SUGAR IS A BROWN SUGAR WITH A CARAMEL FLAVOR. IT IS SOLD IN BLOCKS—
A GOOD SUBSTITUTE IS DARK BROWN SUGAR.

Heat the wok, add 2 tablespoons of the oil, and gently stir-fry the garlic, ginger, and chiles for 1 minute. Add the peanuts and stir-fry for 4 to 5 minutes or until the peanuts are golden. Add the sugar and the broth, bring to a boil, and simmer for 5 minutes.

Remove from the heat, cool slightly, then transfer to a food processor and blend to form a purée. Set aside. Wipe the wok clean.

Heat the wok again, add the remaining oil, and stir-fry the chicken for 3 minutes or until sealed. Add the peanut sauce and the lime juice and cook for 4 to 6 minutes, stirring until the chicken is thoroughly cooked. Sprinkle with the chile and serve with the lime wedges.

Serves **4**
Preparation time **10 minutes**
Cooking time **20 minutes**

3 Tbsp oil
1 garlic clove, peeled and crushed
One 1-in piece gingerroot, peeled and grated
1 to 2 bird's eye chiles, seeded and chopped
4 oz raw shelled peanuts

2 tsp palm sugar or dark brown sugar
1¼ cups chicken or vegetable broth
1 lb boneless, skinless chicken breast fillets, cut into small cubes
2 Tbsp lime juice

TO SERVE
Sliced red chile and lime wedges

SWEET-AND-SOUR CHICKEN
WITH FRIED RICE

THIS IS QUITE A SUBSTANTIAL DISH AND UNLIKE SOME OF THE OTHER RECIPES, IT DOES NOT NEED MANY ACCOMPANYING DISHES. ONE THAT WOULD BE GOOD WITH THIS IS STIR-FRIED CUCUMBER (SEE PAGE 91).

Cook the rice in 2½ cups lightly salted water for 12 minutes, or until the rice is tender. Drain and set aside.

Heat the wok and add 1 tablespoon of the oil. When hot, stir-fry the chicken for 2 to 3 minutes or until sealed.

Add the carrot and green bell pepper and continue to stir-fry for 2 minutes. Stir in the pineapple, honey, sweet chile sauce, vinegar, and soy sauce. Continue to stir-fry for another 2 minutes or until the chicken is done. Remove from the wok and set aside.

Wipe the wok clean if necessary. Add the remaining oil to the wok, and add the cooked rice with the peas and red bell pepper. Cook for 3 to 4 minutes or until hot. Return the chicken to the wok with the scallions. Heat through, stirring, for 2 minutes or until piping hot, and serve immediately.

Serves **4**
Preparation time **10 minutes**
Cooking time **23 to 25 minutes**

1 cup long-grain rice

Salt to taste

2 Tbsp peanut oil

12 oz fresh chicken stir-fry strips

1 large carrot, peeled and diced

1 green bell pepper, seeded
  and chopped

4 slices fresh or canned
  pineapple, chopped

2 Tbsp honey, warmed

1 to 2 Tbsp sweet chile sauce,
  or to taste

3 Tbsp rice wine vinegar or white
  wine vinegar

2 Tbsp dark soy sauce

¾ cup frozen peas

1 small red bell pepper, seeded and
  chopped fine

6 scallions, trimmed and chopped

CHICKEN WITH SPICED YOGURT SAUCE

ADDING THE GROUND ALMONDS AT THE END OF THE COOKING TIME
HELPS TO THICKEN THE SAUCE AS WELL AS GIVING A SLIGHT NUTTY FLAVOR.

Heat the wok, add 1 tablespoon of the oil, and stir-fry the chicken for 3 to 4 minutes or until sealed. Remove from the wok and set aside.

Reheat the wok. Add the remaining oil, and stir-fry the onion, garlic, and chiles for 1 minute. Return the chicken to the wok, add the spices, and continue to stir-fry for 1 minute.

Add the broth and cook for 5 minutes before adding the yogurt and ground almonds. Heat gently for 2 to 3 minutes, stirring frequently, then sprinkle with the chopped cilantro and almonds. Garnish with lemon wedges and serve with rice.

Serves **4**
Preparation time **5 minutes**
Cooking time **14 minutes**

2 Tbsp oil
1 lb boneless, skinless chicken breasts, cut into strips
1 onion, peeled and cut into wedges
3 to 4 garlic cloves, peeled and sliced thin
2 green jalapeño chiles, seeded and chopped
1 tsp ground cumin
1 tsp ground coriander
6 green cardamom pods, bruised
⅔ cup chicken broth
⅔ cup low-fat, plain yogurt
2 Tbsp ground almonds
2 Tbsp chopped fresh cilantro
1 Tbsp toasted sliced almonds

TO GARNISH
Lemon wedges

TO SERVE
Freshly cooked rice

ASIAN-STYLE CHICKEN

MIRIN IS A RICE WINE USED FOR COOKING, NOT DRINKING.
IT ADDS A SWEET FLAVOR. IF UNAVAILABLE, USE SHERRY.

Serves **4**
Preparation time **10 minutes plus 30
minutes marinating time**
Cooking time **40 minutes**

**One 3-lb chicken, jointed into
8 portions**
1 Tbsp mirin or dry sherry
2 Tbsp dark soy sauce
1 tsp dried crushed chiles
**One 1-in piece gingerroot,
peeled and chopped**
**2 tsp roasted seasoning
(see page 25)**
2 tsp palm or dark brown sugar

FOR THE SAUCE
2 Tbsp Chinese chile sauce
3 Tbsp light soy sauce
1 Tbsp sesame oil
1 tsp honey, warmed
2 Tbsp mirin or dry sherry

TO SERVE
**Stir-fried red and green bell pepper
strips and shredded scallions**

Remove and discard the chicken skin, score the flesh, and set aside. Blend
the mirin or sherry, soy sauce, dried crushed chiles, ginger, seasoning, and
sugar, and rub over the chicken portions. Leave in the refrigerator for at least
30 minutes, longer if time permits.

Place either a steamer or a rack in the wok and add 2 inches of water. Arrange
the chicken on an ovenproof plate and bring the water to a boil. Cover the wok
tightly with either a lid or foil and gently steam the chicken for about 30 minutes,
or until it is tender. Add more water to the wok if required.

Just before cooking, combine all the ingredients for the sauce and set aside.

Serve with the sauce, bell peppers, and scallions.

Asian-style Chicken

MARINATED STIR-FRY CHICKEN

THAI BASIL IS DARKER THAN ITS EUROPEAN COUNTERPART AND THE FLAVOR IS MORE EARTHY. IF UNAVAILABLE, USE ORDINARY BASIL.

Serves **4**
Preparation time **10 minutes plus**
   30 minutes marinating time
Cooking time **9 minutes**

12 oz boneless, skinless chicken breasts
½ to 1 tsp dried crushed chiles
2 Tbsp olive oil
3 Tbsp orange juice
A few sprigs of fresh basil
1 Tbsp peanut oil

1 red onion, peeled and cut into wedges
1 red bell pepper, seeded and cut into
   small chunks
One 14-oz can artichoke hearts, drained
   and cut in half
Assorted bitter salad leaves,
   such as watercress, arugula,
   and mustard greens

Trim the chicken and cut into cubes. Place in a shallow dish and sprinkle with the dried crushed chiles. Blend the olive oil with the orange juice and pour over the chicken. Chop a few sprigs of basil and scatter them over the chicken. Stir, then cover and marinate in the refrigerator for 30 minutes.

Heat the wok and add the peanut oil. Stir-fry the onion and bell pepper for 2 minutes. Remove from the wok with a slotted spoon.

Drain the chicken, reserving the marinade, and stir-fry for 3 minutes. Return the red onion and bell pepper to the wok with the marinade and artichoke hearts. Stir-fry for 2 to 3 minutes, or until the chicken is done. Arrange on the salad leaves and serve.

SIZZLING CHICKEN WITH CASHEWS

MARINATING CHICKEN OR ANY POULTRY IN BEATEN EGG WHITE AND CORNSTARCH TENDERIZES THE MEAT REALLY QUICKLY, AND TRANSFORMS THE TASTE AND ENJOYMENT OF THE DISH.

1 large egg white

1 Tbsp cornstarch

1 lb chicken stir-fry strips

2 Tbsp peanut oil

1 green serrano chile, seeded and chopped

3 garlic cloves, peeled and sliced thin

¾ cup cashews

2 Tbsp light soy sauce

2 Tbsp chopped fresh chile

TO SERVE

Freshly cooked Thai fragrant rice

Beat the egg white and cornstarch together in a medium sized bowl. Add the chicken strips and stir until coated. Cover and leave in the refrigerator for 30 minutes.

When ready to cook, heat the wok until hot and add 1 tablespoon of the oil. Heat for 30 seconds, then stir-fry the chile and garlic for 1 minute.

Heat the remaining oil, add the chicken strips to the wok, and stir-fry for 3 minutes. Add the cashews and continue to stir-fry for 2 to 3 minutes, or until the chicken is done.

Add the soy sauce and stir lightly. Sprinkle with the chopped chile and serve immediately with rice.

DEEP-FRIED SHREDDED DUCK

THIS DISH IS ABSOLUTELY DELICIOUS AND EXTREMELY QUICK TO PREPARE.

Serves **4**

Preparation time **8 to 10 minutes**

Cooking time **3 to 6 minutes**

12 oz boneless, skinless duck breasts

1 Tbsp hot chile sauce

1 Tbsp hoisin sauce

4 Tbsp plum sauce

1 Tbsp sesame oil

1 medium egg

1 large carrot, peeled and
  cut into thin matchsticks

1 green bell pepper, seeded
  and cut into thin strips

3 Tbsp cornstarch

1¼ cups oil for deep-frying

FOR THE DIPPING SAUCE

3 Tbsp plum sauce

1 Tbsp light soy sauce

1 tsp hot chile sauce or to taste

1 bird's eye chile, seeded
  and chopped fine

TO GARNISH

Diagonally sliced scallions

TO SERVE

**Freshly cooked stir-fried
  vegetables and noodles**

Cut the duck into fine shreds and set aside. Place all the other ingredients, except the oil for deep-frying, in a large bowl and stir until blended. Stir in the shredded duck.

Heat the oil in the wok to 375°F and deep-fry spoonfuls of the mixture in the hot oil for 1 to 2 minutes, breaking up with a spoon to keep the shreds separate. Drain thoroughly. (Do this in 2 to 3 batches.)

Blend the dipping sauce ingredients together. Garnish the duck with scallions and serve with stir-fried vegetables, noodles, and dipping sauce.

STIR-FRIED DUCK WITH PLUM SAUCE

CHINESE FIVE-SPICE POWDER IS A BLEND OF STAR ANISE, SZECHUAN PEPPERCORNS, FENNEL, CLOVES, AND CINNAMON. IT WILL KEEP INDEFINITELY IN A SEALED JAR IN A COOL DARK PLACE.

Serves **4**
Preparation time **10 minutes plus**
   30 minutes marinating time
Cooking time **25 minutes**

4 duck breasts
2 Tbsp soy sauce
1 tsp Chinese five-spice powder
4 Tbsp orange juice

1 lb fresh plums, pitted and quartered
1 cinnamon stick, bruised
3 Tbsp light brown sugar
2 Tbsp white wine vinegar
1 Tbsp oil

TO SERVE
Warmed Chinese pancakes, shredded
   scallions, and cucumber

Discard the skin from the duck breasts. Cut into very thin strips and place in a shallow dish. Blend the soy sauce, Chinese five-spice powder, and orange juice, then pour over the duck. Cover and let stand in the refrigerator for 30 minutes.

Rinse the plums and place in the wok with the cinnamon stick, sugar, vinegar, and ⅔ cup water. Bring to a boil and then simmer for 20 minutes, or until done. Cool and blend to a smooth purée in a food processor. If necessary, pass through a fine sieve to remove any lumps. Set aside.

Wipe the wok clean, then heat. When hot, add the oil. Drain the duck and stir-fry for 3 to 5 minutes, or until done to personal preference. Serve with the warmed pancakes, the shredded scallions and cucumber, and the plum dipping sauce.

Stir-fried Duck with Plum Sauce

TOM YUM SUPPER

THIS SOUPLIKE DISH IS SO FILLING THAT IT MAKES AN IDEAL LUNCH OR SUPPER. SERVE WITH SOME WARM STRIPS OF PITA OR CRUSTY BREAD.

Serves **4**
Preparation time
   8 to 10 minutes
Cooking time **22 to 23 minutes**

8 oz boneless, skinless chicken breasts
1 quart chicken broth
¾ cup long-grain rice
1 bird's eye chile, seeded and chopped
2 lemon grass stalks, chopped, outer
   leaves discarded

2 to 3 Tbsp red chile paste (see page 12)
1 red bell pepper, seeded
   and shredded fine
1 large carrot, peeled and cut
   into julienne strips
2 Tbsp lime juice
1 to 2 tsp palm or dark brown sugar
4 oz bean sprouts
1 Tbsp shredded fresh basil leaves

Cut the chicken into thin shreds and set aside. Place the broth in a wok with the rice, chile, and lemon grass and simmer for 15 minutes. Blend the chile paste with a little of the hot broth and stir into the wok together with the chicken, red bell pepper, carrot, and lime juice.

Simmer the chicken for 5 minutes, then stir in the remaining ingredients (except the basil) and simmer for 2 to 3 minutes, or until piping hot. Serve in large bowls, sprinkled with the shredded basil.

TURKEY WITH CRANBERRIES
AND SHIITAKE MUSHROOMS

IF FRESH OR FROZEN CRANBERRIES ARE UNAVAILABLE, USE 3 TO 4 TABLESPOONS OF STORE-BOUGHT CRANBERRY SAUCE, PREFERABLY ONE THAT INCLUDES WHOLE CRANBERRIES.

¾ cup fresh or defrosted frozen cranberries

1 to 2 Tbsp dark brown sugar, or to taste

1 lb turkey stir-fry strips

⅔ cup cranberry juice

2 Tbsp dark soy sauce

1 Tbsp grated orange zest

1 Tbsp peanut oil

2 garlic cloves, peeled and crushed

1½ cups shiitake mushrooms, wiped and halved

4 oz sugar snap peas

Place the cranberries and sugar in the wok with 3 to 4 tablespoons water and cook gently for 10 minutes or until the cranberries "pop." Remove from the wok and set aside. (Add sufficient sugar to sweeten slightly while still leaving some tartness.) Wipe the wok clean.

Place the turkey stir-fry strips in a shallow dish. Blend the cranberry juice with the soy sauce and orange zest and pour over the turkey. Cover and marinate in the refrigerator for at least 30 minutes.

When ready to cook, heat the wok and add the oil. Stir-fry the garlic for 1 minute. Drain the turkey, reserving 2 tablespoons of the marinade. Add the turkey to the wok and stir-fry for 2 minutes.

Add the mushrooms and sugar snap peas to the wok with the reserved marinade and stir-fry for 2 minutes. Add the cooked cranberries and stir-fry for 1 minute, or until the turkey is done and the cranberries are hot. Serve immediately.

TWICE-COOKED TURKEY WITH
ASPARAGUS AND MUSHROOMS

THERE ARE MANY VARIETIES OF NOODLES FROM WHICH TO CHOOSE. I WOULD THOROUGHLY RECOMMEND THAT YOU BUY A SELECTION TO TRY. FOR THIS DISH, A BROAD RIBBON EGG NOODLE IS IDEAL.

Serves **4**

Preparation time **8 to 10 minutes**

Cooking time **8 to 10 minutes**

1 lb turkey breast steaks

⅔ cup turkey or chicken broth

2 Tbsp peanut oil

1 red bell pepper, seeded and sliced

6 oz asparagus spears,
cut into 3-in lengths

1½ cups shiitake mushrooms,
wiped and halved

1½ cups oyster mushrooms, wiped
and halved

5 Tbsp yellow bean sauce

2 Tbsp light soy sauce

1 Tbsp hot chile sauce, or to taste

1 Tbsp chopped fresh cilantro

TO SERVE

Freshly cooked noodles

Cut the turkey into thin strips. Place the broth in the wok and bring to a boil. Add the turkey and cook gently for 3 minutes. Remove from the heat, drain, and set aside.

Wipe the wok clean and reheat, then add the oil. When hot, add the drained turkey and stir-fry for 2 to 3 minutes before adding the bell pepper, asparagus, and mushrooms. Stir-fry for 2 minutes. Add the yellow bean, soy, and hot chile sauces.

Stir-fry for 1 to 2 minutes, or until the turkey is done. Sprinkle with the cilantro and serve with noodles.

CHICKEN WITH SESAME SEEDS

THERE ARE MANY VARIETIES OF RICE WINE VINEGAR USED IN ASIAN COOKING.
THEY RANGE IN FLAVOR FROM SPICY AND TART TO SWEET AND PUNGENT.

Cut the chicken into fine shreds, then beat together the egg white and cornstarch. Pour the mixture over the chicken and stir lightly until coated. Cover and leave in the refrigerator for at least 30 minutes.

Cut the bell peppers into fine strips and set aside.

When ready to cook, heat the wok and add 2 tablespoons of the peanut oil. Add the chicken and stir-fry for 2 to 3 minutes, or until the chicken becomes white. Remove from the wok and set aside. Wipe the wok clean if necessary. Add the remaining oil and the bell peppers and stir-fry for 1 minute.

Remove with a slotted spoon and set aside.

Reheat the wok and add the sesame oil. Stir-fry the sesame seeds for 1 minute, or until golden. Add all the sauce ingredients and cook for 1 to 2 minutes, stirring frequently.

Return the chicken and bell peppers to the wok. Stir-fry for 2 minutes, or until the chicken is done.

Serve the chicken with the sauce.

Serves **4**
Preparation time **10 minutes**
   plus 30 minutes marinating time
Cooking time **10 minutes**

1 lb chicken stir-fry strips
1 large egg white, beaten
1 Tbsp cornstarch
1 red bell pepper, seeded
1 orange bell pepper, seeded

3 Tbsp peanut oil
1 tsp sesame oil
1 Tbsp sesame seeds

FOR THE SAUCE
1 Tbsp light soy sauce
1 to 2 tsp hot chile sauce
2 tsp honey, warmed
1 tsp rice wine vinegar
   or sherry vinegar

LEMON CHICKEN

TO BRUISE LEMON GRASS, ROLL ALONG ITS LENGTH WITH A ROLLING PIN UNTIL THE STALKS ARE SLIGHTLY CRUSHED. THIS RELEASES ITS WONDERFUL CITRUS AROMA.

Place the broccoli florets in a small bowl. Cover with boiling water, let stand for 5 minutes, then drain and set aside.

Cut the chicken into bite-size cubes and place in a shallow dish. Blend 2 tablespoons of the lemon juice with the cornstarch and pour over the chicken. Stir lightly until the chicken is coated. Cover and let stand for 30 minutes in the refrigerator.

When ready to cook, heat the wok and add 2 tablespoons of the oil. Add the chicken and stir-fry for 2 minutes, or until the chicken is white. Remove from the wok and wipe the wok clean.

Return the wok to the heat. When hot, add the remaining oil and stir-fry the chile and lemon grass for 1 minute. Return the chicken to the wok with the broccoli and continue to stir-fry for 2 minutes. Add the remaining lemon juice, soy sauce, rice wine or sherry, the scallion, and the pine nuts and stir-fry for 2 minutes, or until the chicken is thoroughly cooked. Discard the lemon grass stalks and serve immediately, garnished with the lemon zest.

Serves **4**
Preparation time **10 minutes**
   plus 30 minutes marinating time
Cooking time **7 minutes**

8 oz broccoli florets
1 lb boneless, skinless
   chicken pieces
4 Tbsp lemon juice
1 Tbsp cornstarch
3 Tbsp peanut oil
1 bird's eye chile, seeded
   and sliced

2 lemon grass stalks, bruised
2 Tbsp light soy sauce
2 Tbsp rice wine or
   medium-dry sherry
6 scallions, trimmed and
   diagonally sliced
2 Tbsp toasted pine nuts

TO GARNISH
Grated lemon zest

SZECHUAN TURKEY STIR-FRY

GINGERROOT CAN BE PREPARED IN SEVERAL DIFFERENT WAYS. YOU CAN GRATE THE GINGER ON THE COARSE SIDE OF A GRATER WITHOUT PEELING IT FIRST, OR YOU CAN PEEL IT AND PASS IT THROUGH A GARLIC PRESS, OR SIMPLY SHRED IT VERY FINE. WHATEVER YOUR PREFERENCE, THERE'S NO SURPASSING THE FRESH, TANGY FLAVOR IT IMPARTS TO ANY DISH IN WHICH IT IS USED.

Cut the turkey into thin strips and place in a shallow dish. Scatter with ginger, garlic, and chile. Pour in the vinegar, stir well, cover, and marinate in the refrigerator for 30 minutes. Stir occasionally during this time.

Heat the wok and add the oil. When hot, stir-fry the turkey for 2 to 3 minutes or until sealed. Add the carrot and sugar snap peas and continue to stir-fry for another 2 minutes.

Blend the black bean sauce with the sweet chile sauce and honey, and stir the mixture into the wok. Continue to cook, stirring, for 2 to 3 minutes, or until the turkey is done. Sprinkle with the shredded scallions and serve with fried rice.

Serves **4**
Preparation time **8 minutes plus 30 minutes marinating time**
Cooking time **6 to 8 minutes**

1 lb turkey breast
One 1-in piece gingerroot, peeled and grated
3 garlic cloves, peeled and sliced
1 red serrano chile, seeded and chopped
1 Tbsp rice vinegar
1 Tbsp peanut oil
1 large carrot, peeled and cut into ribbons
6 oz sugar snap peas
4 Tbsp black bean sauce
1 to 2 Tbsp sweet chile sauce to taste
1 tsp honey

TO GARNISH
Shredded scallions

TO SERVE
Freshly cooked fried rice

VEGETABLES

MUSHROOM AND SUGAR SNAP PEA STIR-FRY

THIS MAKES AN IDEAL SIDE VEGETABLE DISH. FOR A MORE SUBSTANTIAL MEAL, STIR-FRY SOME DRAINED, CUBED TOFU (BEAN CURD) WITH THE GARLIC AND CHILE, THEN PROCEED AS BELOW.

Cover the dried mushrooms with almost-boiling water and let stand for 20 minutes before draining. Cut the wild and closed-cup mushrooms in half or quarters, depending on their size, then rinse very lightly and pat dry on paper towels.

Heat the wok and add the oil. When hot, stir-fry the garlic and chile for 1 minute. Add the orange bell pepper and stir-fry for 1 minute before adding the mushrooms, including the soaked and drained mushrooms. Continue to stir-fry for 3 minutes. Add the sugar snap peas and stir-fry for 1 minute.

Add the soy and black bean sauces, stir-fry for 2 minutes, and add the scallions and sesame oil. Stir-fry for 1 minute, or until the vegetables are tender, and serve with the rice.

Serves **4**
Preparation time **10 minutes**
  plus 20 minutes soaking time
Cooking time **9 minutes**

1/4 cup dried cep mushrooms
3 cups assorted wild mushrooms
1 1/2 cups closed cup mushrooms
1 Tbsp oil
4 garlic cloves, peeled and sliced
1 red serrano chile, seeded
  and chopped
1 orange bell pepper, seeded and
  sliced into half-moon shapes
8 oz sugar snap peas
2 Tbsp dark soy sauce
4 Tbsp black bean sauce
8 baby scallions, trimmed
1 tsp sesame oil

TO SERVE
Freshly cooked Thai fragrant rice

STIR-FRIED BROCCOLI
WITH HOISIN SAUCE

WHEN STIR-FRYING BROCCOLI, IT IS A GOOD IDEA TO BLANCH THE BROCCOLI FIRST IN BOILING WATER
SO THAT IT IS COOKED AND TENDER AT THE END OF THE STIR-FRYING TIME.

Cover the broccoli with boiling water and let stand for 5 minutes, then drain and pat dry with paper towels. Cut the orange flesh into segments and set aside.

Heat the wok and add the oil. When hot, add the onion and garlic and stir-fry for 2 minutes.

Add the red bell pepper and broccoli and continue to stir-fry for 4 minutes. Blend the hoisin sauce with 2 tablespoons water. Stir into the wok and continue to stir-fry for 1 to 2 minutes, or until the broccoli is tender.

Sprinkle in the pine nuts and add the orange segments, give a final stir, and serve.

Serves **4 as an accompaniment**
Preparation time **5 minutes plus**
  5 minutes resting time
Cooking time **8 minutes**

12 oz broccoli florets
1 large orange
1 Tbsp oil
1 red onion, peeled and cut into wedges
2 garlic cloves, peeled and sliced
1 red bell pepper, seeded and sliced thin
2 Tbsp hoisin sauce
2 Tbsp toasted pine nuts

STIR-FRIED CABBAGE
WITH SESAME AND GARLIC

COOKING CABBAGE IN THIS WAY KEEPS IT CRISP. COMBINED WITH THE SHALLOTS, GARLIC, AND CHILE, IT MAKES A FLAVORFUL ACCOMPANIMENT TO BROILED, PAN-FRIED, OR OVEN-BAKED FOODS.

Heat the wok and add 2 teaspoons of the sesame oil. Stir-fry the sesame seeds for 1 to 2 minutes, or until golden. Remove from the wok and set aside.

Cut the bread into small cubes. Reheat the wok and add 2 tablespoons of the oil. Stir-fry the bread cubes for 2 to 3 minutes or until golden; remove from the wok and drain on paper towels.

Wipe the wok clean, reheat, and add a further tablespoon of the oil. Stir-fry the garlic, chile, and shallots for 2 minutes. Add the shredded cabbage and stir-fry for 4 minutes, or until almost tender.

Add the remaining sesame oil to the wok, continue to stir-fry for 1 minute, and sprinkle in the reserved sesame seeds and bread croutons. Heat for 30 seconds and serve.

Serves **4**
Preparation time **8 minutes**
Cooking time **10 to 12 minutes**

4 Tbsp sesame oil
2 Tbsp sesame seeds
2 slices white bread
3 to 4 garlic cloves, peeled and sliced
1 red jalapeño chile, seeded and
   chopped
3 shallots, peeled and cut into
   thin wedges
1 small green cabbage such as Savoy,
   shredded fine

EGGPLANT WITH SHIITAKE MUSHROOMS

SHIITAKE MUSHROOMS ARE AROMATIC BLACK MUSHROOMS THAT ADD A UNIQUE FLAVOR TO MEAT AND FISH DISHES. THEY CAN BE BOUGHT DRIED AS WELL AS FRESH, IF DRIED, THEY NEED TO BE SOAKED FOR AT LEAST 15 MINUTES BEFORE USING.

Serves **4**
Preparation time **10 minutes**
Cooking time **15 minutes**

3 Tbsp oil
1 large onion, peeled and cut into wedges
3 garlic cloves, peeled and sliced
1 red serrano chile, seeded and chopped
1 lb eggplant, trimmed and diced
1 red bell pepper, seeded and sliced
  into half-moon shapes
1½ cups shiitake mushrooms,
  wiped and sliced if large
1 zucchini, trimmed and sliced
2 Tbsp dark soy sauce
2 Tbsp mirin or dry sherry

Heat the wok and add 2 tablespoons of the
oil. Stir-fry the onion, garlic, and chile for
2 minutes.

Add the eggplant and stir-fry for 5 minutes over
a moderate heat. Add the remaining oil, the red
bell pepper, mushrooms, zucchini, soy sauce, and
mirin or dry sherry, and continue to stir-fry for
8 minutes, or until the eggplant is tender.
Serve hot.

STIR-FRIED CUCUMBER

COOKED CUCUMBER IS AS DELICIOUS AS RAW.

Serves **4**
Preparation time **10 minutes plus**
  30 minutes marinating time
Cooking time **5 to 6 minutes**

2 large cucumbers
2 tsp salt
1 Tbsp peanut oil
1 bird's eye chile, seeded
  and chopped

1 to 2 garlic cloves,
  peeled and chopped
7 oz bok choy, shredded
4 to 5 Tbsp black bean sauce
8 scallions, trimmed and
  diagonally sliced
1 tsp sesame seeds

Peel the cucumbers, cut in half lengthwise, and scoop out and discard
the seeds. Slice into ¼-inch slices. Place in a colander and sprinkle with
the salt. Let stand for 30 minutes, rinse in cold water, and pat dry on
paper towels.

Heat the wok and add the oil. Stir-fry the chile and garlic for 2 minutes.
Add the cucumber, stir-fry for 1 minute, then stir in the bok choy and
stir-fry for another minute.

Blend the black bean sauce with 2 tablespoons water and stir into the
wok. Stir-fry for 1 to 2 minutes, or until the bok choy has wilted.

Sprinkle with the scallions and sesame seeds and serve.

DEEP-FRIED BEANS AND ASPARAGUS

THE BEANS AND ASPARAGUS HAVE A CHEWY TEXTURE AND
WHEN SERVED IN THIS THICK, AROMATIC SAUCE THEY MAKE
A REALLY DIFFERENT BUT DELICIOUS DISH.

Serves **4 as an accompaniment**
Preparation time **5 minutes plus**
   5 minutes soaking time
Cooking time **10 minutes**

8 oz green beans, trimmed and cut in half
8 oz baby asparagus spears, trimmed
   and cut in half

About 1¼ cups oil for deep-frying
2 garlic cloves, peeled and chopped
1 to 2 green jalapeño chiles,
   seeded and chopped
One 2-in piece gingerroot,
   peeled and grated
4 Tbsp yellow bean sauce
1 Tbsp dry sherry

Cover the beans and asparagus with boiling water, let stand for 5 minutes, then
drain and pat dry.

Heat the oil in the wok to 350°F. Deep-fry the beans and asparagus in small
batches for 2 minutes. Remove from the wok with a slotted draining spoon and
drain thoroughly on paper towels.

Drain the oil from the wok, reserving 1 tablespoon, then wipe the wok clean. Add
the oil and stir-fry the garlic, chiles, and ginger for 1 minute. Add the fried beans
and asparagus to the wok.

Blend the yellow bean sauce with 2 tablespoons water and pour it into the wok with
the sherry. Cook for 1 to 2 minutes, or until the vegetables are hot. Serve immediately.

Deep-fried Beans and Asparagus

THAI VEGETABLE CURRY

VARY THE TYPE OF SQUASH USED IN THIS CURRY DISH
DEPENDING ON WHICH SQUASHES ARE AVAILABLE.

Serves **4**
Preparation time **10 minutes**
Cooking time **19 to 20 minutes**

1 Tbsp peanut oil

1 onion, peeled and cut into wedges

1 lb sweet potatoes, peeled and cubed

10 oz pumpkin, peeled and cubed

1 red bell pepper, seeded and chopped

1 large zucchini, trimmed and
   cut into thick chunks

2 Tbsp red chile paste

2 cups coconut milk

1 Tbsp dark brown sugar

2 Tbsp dark soy sauce

2 Tbsp lime juice

TO GARNISH

Shredded fresh basil leaves

TO SERVE

Freshly cooked Thai rice

Heat the wok and add the oil. When hot, stir-fry the onion, sweet potato, and pumpkin for 4 minutes, until the onion has begun to soften. Add the red bell pepper and zucchini and continue to cook for 2 minutes.

Blend the chile paste with the coconut milk and add to the wok with the sugar and soy sauce. Bring to a boil and simmer for 10 minutes, or until the vegetables are almost tender.

Add the lime juice and continue to simmer for 3 to 4 minutes, or until the vegetables are tender. Sprinkle with the shredded basil leaves and serve with the rice.

WILTED SPINACH WITH GARLIC

FISH SAUCE, AN ESSENTIAL THAI SEASONING, IS A CLEAR BROWN LIQUID, RICH IN PROTEIN AND B VITAMINS. IT IS SALTY WITH A MILD FLAVOR.

Discard any tough stems from the spinach, wash thoroughly, shred, then set aside.

Heat the wok, add the oil, then stir-fry the garlic and chile for 1 minute. Add the spinach and stir-fry for 2 to 3 minutes before adding the tomatoes, scallions, the soy and fish sauces, and sugar. (You may need to add the spinach in two batches; allow the first batch to wilt a little before adding the remainder.)

Continue to stir-fry for 1 to 2 minutes, or until the spinach has wilted, then serve, sprinkled with lemon zest and sliced almonds, if you like.

Serves **4 as an accompaniment**
Preparation time **5 minutes**
Cooking time **6 minutes**

1 lb spinach or red chard

1 Tbsp oil

3 garlic cloves, peeled and sliced thin

1 bird's eye chile, seeded and chopped

3 ripe tomatoes, seeded and chopped

8 scallions, trimmed and sliced

1 Tbsp dark soy sauce

1 Tbsp Thai fish sauce (nam pla)

1 tsp light brown sugar

1 Tbsp zested lemon rind (optional)

2 Tbsp toasted sliced almonds (optional)

NUTTY SPICY GREENS

USE UNSALTED CASHEWS RATHER THAN THE ROASTED SALTED ONES WHICH
WILL ALTER THE TASTE OF THE DISH.

Heat the wok and add 2 tablespoons of the oil. Stir-fry the cashews for 3 to 4 minutes, or until golden. Remove from the wok with a slotted spoon and set aside.

Add 1 tablespoon of the remaining oil to the wok, heat, and add the onion, garlic, ginger, and dried crushed chiles. Stir-fry for 2 minutes.

Add the broccoli, green beans, bell pepper, and mushrooms and stir-fry for 3 minutes. Add the contents of the can of tomatoes, the soy sauce, 2 tablespoons of water, and the roasted seasoning.

Continue to cook for 3 to 4 minutes, or until the vegetables are tender. Sprinkle with the cashews and serve with spoonfuls of sour cream or half-fat crème fraîche.

Serves **4**
Preparation time **10 minutes**
Cooking time **11 to 13 minutes**

3 to 4 Tbsp peanut oil

1 cup unsalted cashews

1 red onion, peeled and sliced

2 to 3 garlic cloves, peeled
   and chopped

One 1-in piece gingerroot,
   peeled and shredded fine

½ to 1 tsp dried crushed chiles

8 oz broccoli florets, blanched

6 oz green beans, trimmed and cut
   into short lengths, blanched

1 orange bell pepper, seeded
   and chopped

1½ cups closed cup mushrooms,
   wiped and halved if large

One 14-oz can chopped tomatoes

1 Tbsp dark soy sauce

1 tsp roasted seasoning
   (see page 24), or to taste

TO SERVE

Sour cream or half-fat
   crème fraîche

LENTIL AND RED PEPPER
STIR-FRY

RICE NOODLES ARE TRADITIONALLY EATEN AS AN ALTERNATIVE TO RICE THROUGHOUT
ASIA AND ARE IDEAL TO USE IN BOTH STIR-FRIES AND SOUPS.

Place the broccoli florets in a bowl and cover with boiling water.
Let stand for 5 minutes, then drain and set aside. Cover the
noodles with boiling water, let stand for 4 minutes, then drain
and set aside.

Heat the wok and add the oil. Stir-fry the ginger, onion, and
garlic for 2 minutes. Add the bell peppers and drained broccoli
and stir-fry for 3 minutes.

Stir in the drained lentils, cashews, soy sauce, hot chile sauce,
and lime zest and juice. Stir-fry for 1 to 2 minutes, or until the
vegetables are tender. Add the noodles and cilantro, stir for
1 minute, then sprinkle with sesame seeds and serve.

Serves **4**
Preparation time **15 minutes plus
9 minutes standing time**
Cooking time **8 to 9 minutes**

10 oz broccoli florets

8 oz stir-fry rice noodles

1 Tbsp oil

**One small piece gingerroot,
peeled and grated**

1 onion, peeled and cut into wedges

3 to 4 garlic cloves, peeled and sliced

2 red bell peppers, seeded and sliced

One 10-oz can green lentils, drained

¼ cup cashews

2 Tbsp dark soy sauce

Few drops hot chile sauce, or to taste

Grated zest and juice of 1 lime

2 Tbsp chopped fresh cilantro

2 Tbsp sesame seeds

RICE AND NOODLES

PORK WITH CRISPY NOODLES

AFTER USING OIL FOR DEEP FRYING, ALLOW TO COOL, STRAIN IT THROUGH A FINE SIEVE TO REMOVE ANY BITS OF FOOD, AND USING A FUNNEL POUR INTO AN EMPTY OIL BOTTLE. SECURE AND LABEL. THIS WAY THE OIL CAN BE USED A FEW TIMES. DO TAKE CARE, HOWEVER, THAT THE OIL IS COOL BEFORE HANDLING.

Soak the noodles in boiling water for 10 minutes, or until soft. Drain and let stand for 10 minutes. (Do this while preparing the meat and vegetables.)

Heat the oil in the wok to 375°F and deep-fry the noodles in small batches, draining on paper towels. Set aside. Strain off the oil and clean the wok.

Heat the wok again and add 1 tablespoon of the strained oil, then stir-fry the garlic, shallots, chile, and ginger for 1 minute. Add a further tablespoon of oil, then add the pork and stir-fry for 3 minutes.

Add the carrots and bell peppers and continue to stir-fry for 2 minutes. Add the yellow bean and soy sauces to the wok and continue to stir-fry for 2 minutes, or until the pork is tender. Serve with the crisp noodles.

Serves **4**
Preparation time **10 minutes**
Cooking time **13 minutes**

6 oz slender egg noodles

2 cups oil for deep-frying

2 garlic cloves, peeled and crushed

4 shallots, peeled and sliced fine

1 serrano chile, seeded and chopped

One 1-in piece gingerroot, peeled and grated

8 oz pork fillet, trimmed and cut into fine shreds

2 carrots, peeled and cut into julienne strips

1 red bell pepper, seeded and cut into thin strips

1 green bell pepper, seeded and cut into thin strips

3 Tbsp yellow bean or black bean sauce

2 Tbsp light soy sauce

EGG-FRIED RICE WITH
CHORIZO SAUSAGE AND SHRIMP

WHEN USING PEELED SHRIMP THAT HAVE ALREADY BEEN COOKED, REHEAT BRIEFLY
AS QUICKLY AS POSSIBLE TO ENSURE THAT THE SHRIMP DO NOT BECOME TOUGH
AND TASTELESS.

Cook the rice in unsalted water for 12 to 15 minutes, or until tender. Drain thoroughly and let stand until cold.

Heat wok and add the oil. When hot, stir-fry the chorizo sausage, Parma ham, and peas for 3 minutes.

Add the cold rice, bean sprouts, and shrimp and stir-fry for 2 minutes, then push to one side of the wok.

Pour the eggs into the base of the wok and stir-fry for 2 minutes over a high heat, or until the eggs have begun to set. Stir in the rice mixture, and continue to cook until the egg has set. Serve immediately, garnished with scallions and pepper.

Serves **4**
Preparation time **8 minutes**
Cooking time **19 to 22 minutes**

½ cup long-grain rice
2 Tbsp oil
6 oz chorizo sausage, diced
2 oz Parma ham, chopped
1 cup frozen peas
4 oz bean sprouts
4 oz peeled shrimp, defrosted if frozen
2 medium eggs, beaten
Salt to taste

TO GARNISH
4 scallions, trimmed and chopped
Freshly ground black pepper

SPICY BEAN THREAD NOODLES

DRIED SHRIMP GIVE TEXTURE AND AN INTENSE FLAVOR TO DISHES. THEY CAN BE FOUND
IN ASIAN SPECIALTY FOOD STORES.

Soak the noodles in boiling water for 4 minutes, drain, and plunge into cold water. Drain again and set aside.

Heat the wok, add 1 tablespoon of the oil, and stir-fry the lemon grass, chiles, and ginger for 1 minute. Add the remaining oil, then add the pork and chicken. Stir-fry for 3 minutes or until sealed.

Add the drained noodles, the fish sauce, sugar, bean sprouts, and lime juice and stir-fry for 4 to 5 minutes, or until the noodles are piping hot.

Add the scallions, cilantro, and ground shrimp if using, and stir-fry for another minute. Serve sprinkled with the peanuts and garnished with the lime wedges.

Serves **4**
Preparation time **10 minutes**
  plus 4 minutes soaking time
Cooking time **9 minutes**

**4 oz cellophane (transparent
  stir-fry) noodles**
2 Tbsp oil
**3 lemon grass stalks, chopped,
  outer leaves discarded**
**1 to 2 bird's eye chiles,
  seeded and chopped**
**One 1-in piece gingerroot,
  peeled and grated**
4 oz lean pork, cut into thin shreds

**4 oz chicken breasts,
  cut into thin shreds**
1 Tbsp Thai fish sauce (nam pla)
1 tsp light brown sugar
4 oz bean sprouts
3 Tbsp lime juice
4 scallions, trimmed and chopped
2 Tbsp chopped fresh cilantro
**1 Tbsp dried ground
  shrimp, optional**
1 Tbsp roasted peanuts, chopped

TO GARNISH
Lime wedges

CHICKEN AND SHRIMP
CHOW MEIN

LIGHT SOY SAUCE IS SALTIER THAN DARK SOY SAUCE AND IS THE BEST ONE TO USE FOR COOKING.

Cook the noodles in plenty of lightly salted boiling water for 4 minutes, or until tender. Drain, plunge into cold water to cool quickly, and set aside.

Shred the chicken into fine strips, place in a shallow dish, and pour over the light soy sauce and rice wine or sherry. Let stand for 10 minutes, drain, and set aside the marinade.

Heat the wok and add the 2 teaspoons of the oil. When hot, stir-fry the chicken for 2 minutes and remove. Add the remaining oil to the wok; when hot add the garlic and stir for 10 seconds. Add the peas and stir until coated with a little oil. Add the drained noodles, shrimp, chicken, reserved marinade, and the dark soy sauce.

Stir-fry for 2 minutes. Add the sesame oil, give a final stir, and serve immediately, sprinkled with chopped chives.

Serves **4**
Preparation time **5 minutes plus**
  10 minutes marinating time
Cooking time **10 minutes**

8 oz medium egg noodles
4 oz boneless, skinless chicken breasts
2 Tbsp light soy sauce
1 Tbsp rice wine or dry sherry
1½ Tbsp oil
1 garlic clove, peeled and crushed
¾ cup peas
3 oz peeled shrimp, defrosted if frozen
1 Tbsp dark soy sauce
1 tsp sesame oil

TO GARNISH
Chopped chives

BEAN CURD WITH
PEPPER TRIO AND RICE

BEAN CURD, OR TOFU, IS USED EXTENSIVELY IN ASIAN COOKING.
IT IS HIGHLY NUTRITIOUS AND RICH IN PROTEIN. IT HAS A BLAND
TASTE BUT EASILY TAKES ON FLAVOR WHEN MARINATED.

Serves **4**
Preparation time **10 minutes**
Cooking time **21 minutes**

¾ **cup long-grain rice**
8 oz tofu (bean curd)
2 Tbsp oil
3 to 4 garlic cloves, peeled
  and crushed
1 red onion, peeled and cut
  into wedges

1 red bell pepper, seeded
  and chopped coarse
1 green bell pepper, seeded
  and chopped coarse
1 yellow bell pepper, seeded
  and chopped coarse
1½ cups oyster mushrooms,
  wiped and chopped coarse
4 Tbsp hoisin sauce

Cook the rice in lightly salted boiling water for 12 minutes or until tender, drain, and set aside. Drain the tofu, cut into cubes, and set aside.

Heat the wok and add 1 tablespoon of the oil. Fry the tofu with the garlic for 2 minutes, then remove the tofu from the wok with a slotted spoon and set aside.

Add the remaining oil to the wok and stir-fry the onion for 1 minute. Add the bell peppers with the mushrooms and stir-fry for 2 minutes before adding the hoisin sauce.

Stir-fry for 1 minute, then return the tofu to the wok with the cooked rice and stir-fry for 3 minutes, or until the vegetables are tender. Serve immediately.

Bean curd with Pepper Trio and Rice

BELL PEPPER, CASHEW, AND SUGAR SNAP PEA CHOW MEIN

THIS MAKES A PERFECT ACCOMPANIMENT TO ANY OF THE DISHES IN THE BOOK OR IS IDEAL AS A MAIN MEAL FOR TWO PEOPLE.

Serves **2 to 4**
Preparation time **8 to 10 minutes**
Cooking time **7 to 9 minutes**

6 oz medium egg noodles

2 Tbsp peanut oil

1 cup unsalted cashews

1 red bell pepper, seeded and chopped

1 yellow bell pepper, seeded and chopped

1 orange bell pepper, seeded and chopped

6 oz sugar snap peas, trimmed and halved

3 Tbsp light soy sauce

1 Tbsp rice wine or dry sherry

1 tsp dark brown sugar

6 scallions, trimmed and chopped

1 tsp sesame oil

Cook the noodles in plenty of boiling water for 4 minutes, or until they are tender. Drain and plunge into cold water to stop them from cooking further. Drain and set aside.

Heat the wok and add 1 tablespoon of the peanut oil. Stir-fry the cashews for 2 to 3 minutes, or until golden. Remove from the wok and set aside.

Add the remaining oil to the wok, stir-fry the bell peppers and sugar snap peas for 4 minutes, and then stir in the noodles.

Blend the soy sauce, rice wine or sherry, and sugar and pour into the wok. Stir-fry for 1 to 2 minutes, or until the noodles are hot. Sprinkle with the scallions and cashews, add the sesame oil, give a final stir, and serve.

SPECIAL FRIED RICE

THIS IS A USEFUL ACCOMPANIMENT FOR MEAT, FISH, OR VEGETABLE DISHES. THERE IS NO HARD AND FAST RULE TO ITS INGREDIENTS—YOU CAN ADD OR SUBTRACT ACCORDING TO PERSONAL PREFERENCE OR WHAT YOU HAVE AVAILABLE.

Serves **4**
Preparation time **5 minutes**
Cooking time **21 to 22 minutes**

1 cup long-grain rice
2 Tbsp peanut oil
2 medium eggs, beaten
1 Tbsp light soy sauce
1 bird's eye chile, seeded and
chopped fine
2 Tbsp bacon, chopped fine
¾ cup peas
4 oz raw shrimp, peeled
½ cup corn kernels, canned or frozen
4 scallions, trimmed and chopped
Freshly ground black pepper

Cook the rice in lightly salted boiling water for 12 minutes, or until tender. Drain and arrange on a baking sheet to dry.

Heat the wok and add 1 tablespoon of the oil. Beat the eggs with the soy sauce and chile, pour into the wok, and cook until set. Remove the set egg, cool, cut into shreds, and set aside.

Wipe the wok clean if necessary, then add the remaining oil to the wok and stir-fry the bacon for 2 minutes.

Add the cooled rice with the peas, shrimp, and corn and stir-fry for 3 minutes. Stir in the scallions and the shredded omelet. Heat for 1 to 2 minutes, or until hot, and serve, sprinkled with black pepper.

FRIED RICE WITH SPICY BEANS

ONCE YOU HAVE ADDED THE EGG, YOU NEED TO STIR THOROUGHLY TO ENSURE THAT THE EGG IS COOKED AND DOES NOT MAKE THE RICE SOGGY.

Serves **4 to 6**
Preparation time **5 minutes**
Cooking time **20 minutes**

¾ cup long-grain rice
Salt
2 Tbsp peanut oil
1 onion, peeled and chopped
2 garlic cloves, peeled
and chopped
1 red serrano chile,
seeded and chopped

1 yellow bell pepper, seeded
and chopped
10 oz canned red kidney beans
½ cup shelled fava beans,
defrosted if frozen
1 medium egg, beaten
1 Tbsp light soy sauce
2 Tbsp chopped fresh cilantro

TO GARNISH
1 tsp paprika

Cook the rice in plenty of lightly salted boiling water for 12 minutes or until tender. Drain and arrange on a baking sheet. Allow to dry.

Heat the wok and add the oil. When hot, stir-fry the onion, garlic, and chile for 2 minutes. Add the yellow bell pepper and stir-fry for 1 minute, then stir in the cold rice, the red kidney beans, and the fava beans. Continue to stir-fry for 3 minutes.

Beat the egg with the soy sauce and pour into the wok. Cook, stirring, for 2 minutes, or until the egg has set. Stir in the cilantro and serve sprinkled with the paprika.

KOREAN CELLOPHANE NOODLES WITH MIXED VEGETABLES

IF FRESH KAFFIR LIME LEAVES ARE UNAVAILABLE, LOOK FOR DRIED ONES, THEN SIMPLY CRUMBLE THEM IN WHEN STIR-FRYING THE GARLIC AND CHILE.

Serves **4**
Preparation time **10 minutes**
Cooking time **8 minutes**

8 oz cellophane (transparent stir-fry) noodles
2 Tbsp peanut oil
1 to 2 bird's eye chiles, seeded and chopped
2 to 4 garlic cloves, peeled and chopped
2 lemon grass stalks, chopped, outer leaves discarded
2 kaffir lime leaves, crushed

One 1-in piece gingerroot, peeled and shredded fine
2 carrots, peeled and diced
4 oz broccoli florets
4 oz cauliflower florets
¾ cup peas
4 oz baby corn
2 Tbsp dark soy sauce
3 Tbsp oyster sauce
1 Tbsp Thai fish sauce (nam pla)
1 tsp dark brown sugar
1 Tbsp chopped fresh basil leaves

Soak the noodles in boiling water for 4 minutes, then drain and set aside.

Heat the wok, add the oil, and stir-fry the chiles, garlic, lemon grass, kaffir lime leaves, and gingerroot for 2 minutes. Add all the vegetables and continue to stir-fry for 3 minutes.

Blend the soy sauce with the oyster and fish sauces, stir in the sugar, and add to the wok. Stir, then add the drained noodles.

Continue to cook, stirring, until the vegetables are done but still crisp and the noodles are hot. Sprinkle with the basil leaves and serve.

ORIENTAL NOODLES

ALTHOUGH I HAVE SUGGESTED USING TRANSPARENT NOODLES FOR THIS DISH, OTHER NOODLES WILL WORK AS WELL. JUST FOLLOW THE PACKAGE INSTRUCTIONS FOR THE LENGTH OF TIME REQUIRED TO SOAK THEM.

Serves **4**
Preparation time **8 minutes**
Cooking time **9 to 11 minutes**

4 oz cellophane (transparent stir-fry) noodles
2 Tbsp peanut oil
1 medium egg, beaten
2 garlic cloves, peeled and chopped
1 bird's eye chile, seeded and chopped

9 oz tofu (bean curd), drained and cubed
2 Tbsp green chile paste (see page 12)
4 oz bean sprouts
1 Tbsp Thai fish sauce
1 Tbsp sweet chile sauce
2 Tbsp dark soy sauce
1 Tbsp chopped fresh cilantro

Cover the noodles with boiling water, let stand for 4 minutes then drain and set aside.

Heat the wok and add 1 tablespoon of the oil. When hot, pour in the beaten egg and cook until set. Remove the set egg from the wok and cut into strips.

Wipe the wok clean if necessary, reheat, then add the remaining oil. Add the garlic and chile and stir-fry for 1 minute. Add the tofu and continue to stir-fry for 2 to 3 minutes, or until golden. Add the green chile paste and stir-fry for another minute. Add the remaining ingredients, except the cilantro and the drained noodles. Stir-fry for 3 to 4 minutes or until piping hot. Sprinkle with the cilantro, add the noodles, and serve.

SALADS

DUCK STRIPS
ON WILTED ARUGULA

THIS RECIPE WILL WORK EQUALLY WELL WITH EITHER CHICKEN OR TURKEY BREAST AND
MAKES AN INTERESTING MAIN-COURSE SALAD.

Remove 1 tablespoon of the zest from one of the oranges
and set aside. Peel the oranges and divide into segments.
Remove the skin (over a bowl in order to catch the juice),
and set aside the segments.

Trim the duck, cut into thin strips, and place in a shallow dish.
Blend the orange juice, vinegar, and honey together and pour
over the duck. Let stand, lightly covered, in the refrigerator for
30 minutes. Stir occasionally during this time.

Heat the wok and add 1 tablespoon of the oil. Drain the duck,
reserving the marinade, then stir-fry for 2 minutes or until
sealed. Remove from the wok and set aside. If necessary, clean
the wok before adding the remaining oil.

Stir-fry the fennel for 2 minutes. Return the duck to the wok
with the reserved marinade and stir-fry for 2 minutes. Add the
sugar snap peas, cherry tomatoes, and arugula or spinach. Stir-
fry for 1 to 2 minutes, until the leaves have begun to wilt.

Add the orange segments and give a final stir. Serve
immediately sprinkled with sliced almonds, with crusty bread
or new potatoes.

Serves **4**
Preparation time **10 minutes plus
30 minutes marinating time**
Cooking time **8 to 10 minutes**

2 large oranges
2 duck breasts (about 8 oz in total)
2 Tbsp orange juice
2 Tbsp balsamic vinegar
1 tsp honey, warmed
2 Tbsp oil
1 fennel head, trimmed and sliced fine
**6 oz sugar snap peas or
mange tout, halved**
½ cup cherry tomatoes, halved
8 oz arugula or baby spinach leaves

TO SERVE
2 Tbsp sliced almonds
**Warm crusty bread or freshly cooked
new potatoes**

WARM TURKEY SALAD WITH JULIENNED VEGETABLES

THE CRISPY LEEKS FOR THE GARNISH ARE EASY TO MAKE. FINELY SHRED THE LEEKS AFTER CLEANING, AND PLUNGE INTO HOT OIL FOR A FEW SECONDS. DRAIN WELL ON PAPER TOWELS.

Serves **4**
Preparation time
   10 minutes plus 30 minutes
   marinating time
Cooking time **9 to 10 minutes**

10 oz fresh turkey breast fillet
1 large egg white
1 Tbsp cornstarch
3 Tbsp oil

1 small red onion, peeled and sliced thin
1 carrot, peeled and cut into thin strips
1 large zucchini, trimmed and
   cut into thin strips
1 orange bell pepper, seeded
   and cut into thin strips
8 oz young leeks, trimmed and shredded
3 Tbsp lemon juice
2 Tbsp dark soy sauce
1 tsp honey

Trim the turkey, cut into thin strips, and place in a shallow dish. Beat the egg white with the cornstarch and pour over the turkey. Cover and marinate in the refrigerator for 30 minutes, stirring occasionally.

Heat the wok and add 2 tablespoons of the oil. Stir-fry the turkey for 3 minutes or until sealed. Remove from the wok and set aside. Clean the wok if necessary.

Add the remaining oil to the wok and stir-fry the onions and carrot for 2 minutes.

Add the remaining vegetables and stir-fry for 2 minutes. Return the turkey to the wok with the lemon juice, soy sauce, and honey. Stir-fry for 1 to 2 minutes, or until the turkey is piping hot. Serve immediately.

Warm Turkey Salad with Julienned Vegetables

STIR-FRIED CRAB AND BOK CHOY SALAD

IF PREFERRED, THE BOK CHOY CAN BE ADDED TO THE WOK AND STIR-FRIED FOR 1 TO 2 MINUTES AT THE END OF THE COOKING TIME. EITHER WAY, THIS DELICATE SALAD IS PERFECT FOR ENTERTAINING.

Serves **4**
Preparation time
  8 to 10 minutes
Cooking time **7 to 9 minutes**

2 Tbsp peanut oil

2 lemon grass stalks, bruised, outer
  leaves discarded

2 kaffir lime leaves

1 red bird's eye chile, seeded
  and chopped

1 large carrot, peeled and cut
  into julienne strips

1 large zucchini, peeled and cut
  into julienne strips

One 7-oz can water chestnuts,
  drained and sliced in half

1 cup unsalted cashews

12 oz white crab meat, drained if canned
  and defrosted if frozen

2 Tbsp light soy sauce

2 Tbsp rice wine or dry sherry

7 oz bok choy, shredded

Heat the wok and add the oil. When hot, stir-fry the lemon grass, kaffir lime leaves, chile, carrot, and zucchini for 3 minutes.

Add the water chestnuts and cashews to the wok. Stir-fry for 2 to 3 minutes, or until the nuts are golden.

Add the crab meat to the wok and stir-fry for 1 minute. Add the soy sauce and rice wine or sherry, heat through for another 1 to 2 minutes, and serve on the shredded bok choy.

SAUTÉED VENISON, ASPARAGUS, AND CHANTERELLE SALAD

IF CHANTERELLE MUSHROOMS ARE UNAVAILABLE, USE OYSTER OR CHESTNUT MUSHROOMS. SLICE THE MUSHROOMS IF THEY ARE LARGE. BEEF FILLET STEAKS CAN REPLACE THE VENISON.

Trim the steak, cut into thin strips, and place in a shallow dish. Blend 2 tablespoons of the oil with the vinegar, soy sauce, and red currant jelly. Pour over the steak. Cover and leave in the refrigerator for 30 minutes, spooning the marinade over occasionally. Drain, reserving 4 tablespoons of the marinade.

Heat the wok and add the remaining oil. Stir-fry the shallots, garlic, and chile for 1 minute. Add the drained steak and stir-fry for 2 minutes, then remove from the wok with a slotted spoon.

Add the asparagus and mushrooms to the wok and stir-fry for 2 minutes. Return the steak and shallots to the wok with the reserved marinade; stir-fry for 2 to 3 minutes or until the steak is tender.

Add the sliced nectarines to the wok, give a final stir, then arrange on top of the radicchio or salad leaves and serve.

Serves **4**
Preparation time **10 minutes plus 30 minutes marinating time**
Cooking time **8 to 10 minutes**

12 oz venison steaks
3 Tbsp oil
4 Tbsp sherry vinegar
1 Tbsp dark soy sauce
1 Tbsp red currant jelly, warmed
4 shallots, peeled and sliced
2 garlic cloves, peeled and crushed
1 red jalapeño chile, seeded and chopped
6 oz baby asparagus spears, cut in half
1½ cups chanterelle mushrooms, wiped, sliced in half if large
2 firm but ripe nectarines, pitted and sliced
Radicchio or assorted salad leaves

PHEASANT WITH TART APPLE AND FRESH MINT

IF PHEASANT BREASTS ARE UNAVAILABLE,
USE DUCK BREASTS OR VENISON STEAKS INSTEAD.

Serves **4**
Preparation time **10 minutes plus**
   30 minutes marinating time
Cooking time **7 minutes**

2 to 3 pheasant breasts
   (about 10 oz in weight)
1 red jalapeño chile, seeded and sliced
²⁄₃ cup apple juice
2 Tbsp chopped fresh mint

1 tsp honey, warmed
2 Tbsp dark soy sauce
2 Tbsp sunflower oil
2 celery stalks, trimmed and sliced thin
1 large tart eating apple (such as Granny
   Smith), peeled, cored, and sliced
8 oz baby spinach leaves, rinsed

TO GARNISH
Fresh mint leaves and pecans

Cut the pheasant into thin strips, place in a shallow dish, and scatter the chile on top. Blend the apple juice with the chopped mint, honey, and soy sauce and pour over the pheasant. Cover and marinate in the refrigerator for at least 30 minutes, turning the strips over occasionally in the marinade.

When ready to cook, drain the pheasant and reserve 2 to 3 tablespoons of the marinade.

Heat the wok until hot and add 1 tablespoon of the oil. When hot, stir-fry the drained strips for 2 minutes. Remove from the wok and set aside.

Add the remaining oil to the wok and stir-fry the celery for 1 to 2 minutes. Add the apple and return the strips to the wok. Stir-fry for 2 minutes.

Add the reserved marinade to the wok with the spinach. Stir-fry for 1 minute or until the strips are tender. Sprinkle with the mint leaves and pecans and serve.

Pheasant with Tart Apple and Fresh Mint

LEEK, BELL PEPPER, AND TOFU SALAD

IT IS IMPORTANT WHEN USING TOFU THAT YOU DRAIN IT FIRST. OTHERWISE IT WILL BE VERY DIFFICULT TO STIR-FRY. TAKE CARE NOT TO OVERCOOK IT.

Serves **4**
Preparation time **10 minutes**
Cooking time **10 to 11 minutes**

2 leeks, trimmed and sliced

9 oz tofu (bean curd)

2 Tbsp peanut oil

1 fennel head, trimmed and thinly sliced

1 red bell pepper, seeded and cut into
  half-moon slices

1 orange bell pepper, seeded
  and cut into half-moon slices

4 oz sugar snap peas, halved

2 Tbsp hoisin sauce

2 Tbsp dark soy sauce

2 Tbsp rice wine or dry sherry

1 Tbsp hot chile sauce

1 tsp honey

1 tsp sesame oil

4 oz bok choy, shredded

4 oz bean sprouts

Cover the leeks in boiling water and let stand for 4 minutes. Drain and set aside.

Drain the tofu and cut into bite-size cubes. Heat the wok and add 1 tablespoon of the oil. Stir-fry the tofu for 2 to 3 minutes, or until golden. Remove, drain on paper towels, and set aside.

Add the remaining oil to the wok. Stir-fry the fennel, drained leeks, and bell peppers for 4 minutes. Add the sugar snap peas and tofu and continue to stir-fry for 2 minutes.

Blend the hoisin, soy sauce, rice wine or sherry, hot chile sauce, and honey, and pour into the wok. Continue to stir-fry for 2 minutes. Add the sesame oil and give a final stir to heat through.

Mix the bok choy and bean sprouts together, spoon over the tofu and vegetable stir-fry, and serve.

TROUT, SPINACH, AND RASPBERRY SALAD

THIS STUNNING SALAD IS IDEAL TO SERVE ON WARM SUNNY DAYS OR BALMY EVENINGS WHEN YOU ARE EATING *AL FRESCO*. SERVE WITH PLENTY OF CHILLED CHARDONNAY, WARM CRUSTY BREAD, AND A MIXED BELL PEPPER SALAD.

Remove the stalks from the parsley, rinse, and pat dry with paper towels. Heat 4 tablespoons of the oil in the wok and fry the parsley in small batches for 30 seconds, or until dark green and crisp. Remove and drain on paper towels.

Wipe the wok clean. Remove as many of the fine bones from the trout fillets as possible and cut into 1-inch strips. (Keep the skin on as this keeps the fish together during cooking.)

Heat the wok and add the oil. When hot, add the trout with the chiles and 1 tablespoon of the lime zest and stir-fry for 2 minutes.

Add the scallions and spinach and stir-fry for 1 minute. Add the vinegar with the pine nuts and continue to stir-fry for 2 minutes, or until the spinach has wilted slightly. Stir in the raspberries and serve immediately, sprinkled with the remaining lime zest and the parsley.

Serves **4**
Preparation time **5 minutes**
Cooking time **6 minutes**

½ **oz curly parsley**
5 **Tbsp oil**
1 **lb trout fillets**
½ **to 1 tsp dried crushed chiles**

2 **Tbsp grated lime zest**
8 **scallions, trimmed and**
   diagonally sliced
8 **oz baby spinach leaves**
1 **Tbsp raspberry vinegar or**
   balsamic vinegar
2 **Tbsp toasted pine nuts**
1 **cup fresh raspberries**

WARM PORK AND MINT SALAD

IT IS IMPORTANT TO BUY GOOD-QUALITY PORK, AND TO CUT IT INTO THIN STRIPS BEFORE MARINATING, TO ENSURE IT IS BEAUTIFULLY TENDER AFTER COOKING.

Serves **4**
Preparation time **10 minutes** plus 30 minutes marinating time
Cooking time **11 minutes**

12 oz pork fillet
2 Tbsp red chile paste
2 Tbsp peanut oil
1 red onion, peeled and sliced thin

1 Tbsp lime juice
1 Tbsp light soy sauce
1 to 2 tsp Thai fish sauce (nam pla)
¾ cup cherry tomatoes
2 red eating apples, cored and sliced
2 Tbsp fresh mint leaves
1 tsp sesame oil

TO SERVE
Bitter salad greens

Cut the pork into thin strips and toss it in the red chile paste. Marinate in the refrigerator for 30 minutes.

Heat the wok and add 1 tablespoon of the oil. Stir-fry the onion for 2 minutes. Remove from the wok and set aside.

Add the remaining oil to the wok and stir-fry the pork for 2 minutes, or until sealed. Return the onion to the wok together with the lime juice and soy and fish sauces and continue to stir-fry for 5 minutes.

Add the cherry tomatoes and sliced apple and stir-fry for another 2 minutes. Add the mint and the sesame oil, give a final stir, then serve on a bed of bitter salad greens.

WARM GADO GADO SALAD

GADO GADO SALADS CAN BE FOUND THROUGHOUT INDONESIA. EVERY VERSION IS DIFFERENT.

Serves **4**
Preparation time **12 minutes**
Cooking time **9 to 10 minutes**

8 oz tofu (bean curd), drained
4 Tbsp peanut oil
1 red onion, peeled and sliced thin
1 to 2 bird's eye chiles, seeded and chopped fine
½ cucumber, cut into thin strips
4 oz green beans, trimmed

6 oz bok choy, shredded
4 Tbsp crunchy peanut butter
4 Tbsp coconut milk or low-fat, plain yogurt
2 Tbsp roasted peanuts

TO GARNISH
2 medium eggs, hard-cooked, shelled, and sliced

Pat the bean curd dry with paper towels and cut into small cubes. Heat the wok, add 2 tablespoons of the oil, and fry the bean curd for 2 to 3 minutes, or until sealed and lightly golden. Remove from the wok and set aside.

Add the remaining oil to the wok and stir-fry the onion and chiles for 2 minutes. Add the cucumber, green beans, and shredded bok choy and stir-fry for 3 minutes. Blend the peanut butter, 4 tablespoons hot water, and the coconut milk or yogurt together until smooth. Add to the wok with the bean curd. Continue to cook for 2 minutes, or until the vegetables are done but still crisp. Sprinkle with the peanuts, garnish with the sliced egg, and serve.

WARM SALMON SALAD

SALMON AND CUCUMBER GO WELL TOGETHER, AND THE ADDITION OF THE FRESH MANGO
GIVES THIS SALAD A DELICIOUS NEW TWIST.

Peel the cucumber, cut in half, then scoop out and discard the seeds. Slice thin and place in a colander, sprinkling with a little salt. Let stand for 20 minutes, rinse thoroughly in cold water, and set aside.

Heat the wok and add 1 tablespoon of oil. Stir-fry the chiles for 1 minute, remove from the wok, and drain on paper towels. Set aside. Cut the salmon into thin strips.

Reheat the wok and add the remaining oil. When hot, stir-fry the mushrooms and bell pepper for 3 minutes. Add the salmon and mango and continue to stir-fry for 2 minutes, or until the salmon is tender.

Stir in the fish, soy, and plum sauces. Add the scallions, the cucumber, and the peanuts. Continue to stir for 1 minute, or until hot. Serve on the spinach leaves, sprinkled with the chopped cilantro and chiles.

Serves **4**
Preparation time **10 minutes**
   plus 20 minutes standing time
Cooking time **7 minutes**

1 large cucumber
1 to 2 Tbsp salt
2 Tbsp peanut oil
2 to 3 red serrano chiles, seeded
   and chopped
12 oz salmon fillets, skinned
1¾ cups oyster mushrooms,
   wiped and sliced
1 red bell pepper, seeded
   and chopped
1 mango, peeled, pitted,
   and chopped
1 Tbsp Thai fish sauce (nam pla)
2 Tbsp light soy sauce
2 Tbsp plum sauce
8 scallions, trimmed and
   diagonally sliced
3 Tbsp roasted peanuts
Baby spinach leaves to serve
1 Tbsp chopped fresh cilantro

DESSERTS

BRANDIED PINEAPPLE

TO CHECK IF A PINEAPPLE IS RIPE, SIMPLY SMELL IT: IF THERE IS A STRONG PINEAPPLE AROMA AND THE LEAVES FROM THE PLUME ARE EASILY REMOVED WHEN LIGHTLY PULLED, THE PINEAPPLE IS READY TO EAT.

Serves **4**
Preparation time **7 minutes**
Cooking time **6 minutes**

1 large just-ripe pineapple
¼ stick butter
3 Tbsp orange juice
3 Tbsp superfine sugar
4 Tbsp brandy
½ cup toasted pecans
Thick Greek yogurt
2 tsp dark brown sugar
Grated orange zest

Discard the plume and skin and cut the pineapple into thick slices. Remove the center core and cut the remainder into chunks.

Heat the butter in the wok and add the pineapple chunks. Cook over a high heat for 1 to 2 minutes, or until the pineapple begins to brown.

Add the superfine sugar to the wok with the brandy and stir-fry until the fruit begins to caramelize.

Sprinkle with the nuts and serve, topped with spoonfuls of yogurt and sprinkled with the dark brown sugar and the orange zest.

FRUITS WITH PASSION FRUIT SAUCE

PASSION FRUITS ARE RIPE WHEN THEY ARE REALLY WRINKLED AND LOOK ALMOST PAST THEIR BEST.

Serves **4**
Preparation time **15 minutes**
Cooking time **10 minutes**

FOR THE PASSION FRUIT SAUCE
½ cup superfine sugar
2 Tbsp Cointreau
3 ripe passion fruits

FOR THE FRUITS
½ stick sweet butter
1 ripe mango, peeled, pitted, and cubed
2 cups strawberries, hulled, cut in half if large
¾ cup seedless red grapes
¾ cup seedless green grapes

TO SERVE
Waffles or pancakes, and ice cream

Place the sugar with ⅔ cup water in the wok and heat gently until the sugar has dissolved. Bring to a boil and boil for 3 minutes. Remove from the heat and stir in the Cointreau. Scoop out the seeds and any juice from the passion fruit and add to the syrup. Set aside until required.

Wipe the wok clean, then add the butter and place over a gentle heat until melted. Add the fruits and gently stir-fry for 3 minutes or until the fruits are heated through. Add the passion fruit sauce, bring to a boil, and serve immediately with ice cream on waffles or pancakes.

TOFFEE APPLES AND BANANAS

THIS DELICIOUS DESSERT IS POPULAR WITH ADULTS AND CHILDREN ALIKE.

Peel, core, and cut the apples into thick slices. Slice the bananas and toss both fruits in the lemon juice.

Blend the flours together. Mix in the egg and about 1 teaspoon of the sesame oil to form a very thick batter.

Heat the peanut oil and the remaining sesame oil in the wok to 375°F. Dip the apples and bananas into the batter, allowing any excess to drip back into the batter. Fry in small batches for 2 minutes, or until golden. Remove and drain on paper towels. Repeat until all the fruit has been fried.

When ready to serve, fill a mixing bowl with cold water and some ice cubes. Reheat the oil to 350°F and fry the fruit again, a few at a time, for another 2 minutes. Drain on paper towels.

Place the sugar, sesame seeds, and 2 tablespoons of the oil from the deep-frying into a heavy-based pan. Place over a moderate heat until the sugar melts and begins to caramelize. Take care not to burn the sugar.

Once the caramel is light golden, add the fried fruits, a few at a time. Stir the fruits in the caramel until they are coated, then remove and plunge into the ice water for a few seconds until the caramel is hard. Remove. Repeat until all the fruits have been used, then serve.

Serves **6**
Preparation time **15 minutes**
Cooking time **20 minutes**

2 firm eating apples
2 firm bananas
2 Tbsp lemon juice
3 Tbsp all-purpose flour
3 Tbsp cornstarch
1 large egg
2 Tbsp sesame oil
1¼ cups peanut oil
¾ cups sugar
2 Tbsp sesame seeds

WARM TROPICAL FRUITS

TO MAKE SHAVINGS OF FRESH COCONUT, SIMPLY CRACK OPEN A FRESH COCONUT; AFTER DRAINING OFF THE MILK, SHAVE OFF THIN STRIPS WITH A VEGETABLE PEELER. THE SHAVINGS CAN BE DRIED AND STORED IN AN AIRTIGHT JAR FOR LATER USE.

Serves **4**
Preparation time **10 minutes**
Cooking time **7 to 8 minutes**

4 Tbsp honey
1 Tbsp light corn syrup
6 star anise
6 oz fresh lychees, peeled and stoned
1 large mango, peeled, pitted, and diced
1 large papaya, peeled, seeded, and diced
2 bananas, peeled and sliced

TO GARNISH
Freshly shaved coconut

TO SERVE
Coconut or vanilla ice cream

Place the honey, syrup, star anise, and 1 cup water in the wok and bring to a boil. Boil gently for 3 minutes. Add all the fruit and heat gently for 3 minutes, or until warm.

Serve immediately, decorated with the shaved fresh coconut and scoops of ice cream.

GINGERED PINEAPPLE

THIS DELICIOUS DESSERT IS EASY AND QUICK TO PREPARE AND IS PERFECT TO SERVE FOR ANY OCCASION.

Serves **4**
Preparation time **5 minutes**
Cooking time **7 minutes**

1 large ripe pineapple
¼ cup superfine sugar
One 2-in piece gingerroot, chopped
¼ cup chopped stem ginger
3 Tbsp ginger syrup (from the stem ginger jar) or ginger wine
3 fresh figs

TO GARNISH
2 tbsp toasted sliced almonds

Discard the plume, skin, and central core from the pineapple and cut into chunks. Set aside.

Place the sugar into the wok with the chopped gingerroot and 1 cup water and bring to a boil. Boil gently for 3 minutes then strain off the gingerroot.

Add the pineapple chunks, the stem ginger, and syrup, and simmer gently for 2 minutes. Cut the figs into quarters, add to the wok, and continue to simmer for another 2 minutes, or until heated through.

Serve sprinkled with the toasted almonds.

SUMMER FRUITS WITH ICED MASCARPONE

THIS DESSERT IS SO SIMPLE TO COOK AND SO DELICIOUS TO EAT. IF TIME IS TIGHT, SIMPLY SERVE THE MASCARPONE IN SPOONFULS WITH THE BERRIES.

Set the freezer to its coldest setting. Beat the cheese with the confectioner's sugar until creamy. Lightly whip the cream until soft peaks form, then fold into the cream cheese together with the Grand Marnier.

Spoon the mixture into a freezable container and freeze for 1 hour (or use an ice-cream maker and follow the manufacturer's instructions). Remove from the freezer, beat, then freeze again for 2 hours. Beat again to break up the ice crystals and return to the freezer for a further 2 hours, or until solid. Allow to soften in the refrigerator for 30 minutes before using.

Heat the superfine sugar with ⅔ cup of water in the wok until the sugar has dissolved. Boil gently for 3 minutes, add the vanilla bean or extract, and simmer for 2 minutes.

Add the fruits to the wok and simmer for 3 minutes. Serve warm with the iced mascarpone, garnished with mint sprigs.

Serves **4**
Preparation time **10 minutes plus 5 hours freezing time**
Cooking time **8 minutes**

One 9-oz tub mascarpone cheese
3 Tbsp confectioner's sugar, sifted
1¼ cups heavy cream
4 Tbsp Grand Marnier
¼ cups superfine sugar
1 vanilla bean or a few
   drops vanilla extract
1 lb mixed summer berries, cleaned

TO GARNISH
Mint sprigs

INDEX